Theorizing Women's Work

Network Foundation for Educational Publishing is a voluntary foundation set up:

1. To facilitate the development of a healthy and responsible Canadian-controlled post-secondary book publishing sector.
2. To assist in the production, dissemination and popularizing of innovative texts and other educational materials for people at all levels of learning.
3. To develop more varied sources for critical works in the Humanities and Social Sciences.
4. To expand the readership for Canadian academic works beyond a select body of scholars.
5. To encourage the academic community to create books on Canadian topics for the community at large.
6. To develop works that will contribute to public information and debate on issues of historical and contemporary concern, thereby improving standards of education and public participation.

The Network Basics Series, one of the Foundation's activities, provides inexpensive books on the leading edge of research and debate to students and the general public.

This Network Basics is published by Garamond Press.
Please direct all enquiries to 67A Portland Street,
Toronto, Ontario M5V 2M9.

Theorizing Women's Work

Pat Armstrong and Hugh Armstrong

**Garamond Press,
Toronto, Canada**

A publication of Garamond Press

Garamond Press 67A Portland Street
Toronto, Ontario M5V 2M9

Copy editing: Irit Shimrat
Design and production: Phoenix Productions
Typesetting: On-line Graphics, Toronto
Printed and bound in Canada

Canadian Cataloguing in Publication Data

Armstrong, Pat, 1945–
  Theorizing Women's Work

(Network basics series)
Includes bibliographical references.
ISBN 0-920059-57-0

1. Women—Employment—Philosophy.
I. Armstrong, Hugh, 1943– . II. Title. III.Series.

HD6053.A75 1990   331.4'01   C90-094145-6

Contents

Preface

The past thirty years have witnessed dramatic changes in women's work. Women have flooded into the labour force. Current estimates indicate that 70 percent of women 15 years of age and over are officially counted as employed or unemployed at some point during the year. Today even women with very young children are increasingly likely to stay in the labour market and to work at full-time paid jobs. Some women have broken into many of the traditionally male strongholds; they are close to becoming the majority in a number of medical and law schools, for example. New technologies and new products have reduced women's domestic workload and increased their control over fertility, at the same time as improving women's chances of surviving childbirth. Women have successfully struggled for legislation on equal pay, on employment equity, on marital and civil rights, on maternity leave and on sexual harassment. They have won affirmative action plans and a guarantee of a place on executive or political committees in many organizations. A growing proportion of women belong to unions, and through them have acquired the right to say no.

But most women remain concentrated in low level clerical, sales, factory and service jobs, doing women's work for women's wages. Women still bear the responsibility for childcare and domestic work. This unpaid work prevents many women from taking on full-time paid employment at the same time as their increasing need for cash is pushing them to take on some kind of paid work. Women still lack safe and effective means of birth control and many of the new technologies have increased men's power in areas related to fertility and birth. Moreover, legislation has had a very limited impact on promotion, pay, harassment or on the distribution of power and household resources. Indeed, to the extent that legislation and other policies have been successful in altering women's condition, they have often served to increase divisions between women rather than to reallocate power or pay between women and men.

How are we to explain this continuity that is combined with dramatic change, this subordination of women as a sex combined with differences among women related to class, race and culture or this success in winning legislation and policies combined with a failure to bring about fundamental alterations in women's work? These are central questions we must answer if we are to alter the nature and conditions of women's work; these are the issues that theory must address if we are to develop adequate strategies for the future.

Our increasingly sophisticated research on women's work has revealed its complexity and diversity, challenging old theories based on simple dichotomies. It has been tempting either to seek refuge in a rejection of any theory that attempts to explain the large picture or to develop intricate theories that are comprehensible only to the initiated. If we are to seek fundamental change, uniting around common purposes that go beyond our immediate situations, it is important to develop explanations at a variety of levels of abstraction. We must develop explanations that are understandable to as many people as possible.

This work is intended to provide a critical overview of English Canadian perspectives on these central questions and to offer a contribution to our ongoing debates about these critical issues. At the same time, it is an argument about the importance of theoretical work and an argument for theory that is accessible.

The book originates from a paper we wrote for a seminar in Yugoslavia, and we have Dean Frease to thank for inviting us to participate. We also have Errol Sharpe of Garamond Press to thank, because he encouraged us to transform that paper into a book. It has been a struggle to carry out what seemed to be a simple task of expansion because we kept facing new complexities and new contributions that had to be addressed. We finally decided to end the process and, as Roberta Hamilton would say, make the draft public, when we saw the book referenced in another text. Peter Saunders, also of Garamond Press, continued to be supportive, even when we continued to revise and reconsider.

The content owes a great deal to the critiques provided by Elaine Bernard, Roberta Hamilton, Meg Luxton and Arlene Steiger. We learned much from Susan Arab, Jackie Choiniere, Niki Cunningham, Jan Kainer, and Ann Porter who discussed the manuscript with us as part of a graduate seminar. We benefitted as well from sessions with other graduate students too numerous to name. While we listened carefully to their advice, they cannot be blamed for what this book contains.

We would also like to thank Irit Shimrat for her prompt, efficient and effective copy-editing work. Finally, we would like to thank our daughters Jill and Sarah, who once again did without their parents' time and put up with our endless, and at times vigorous, conversations about women's work.

Pat Armstrong and Hugh Armstrong
Toronto
April 1990

Chapter One

Theory Counts

Theory is much more than a game academics play. We all carry around in our heads some ideas about how people act and why they act the way they do. These explanations, which are often partial, contradictory, and illogical, filter our interpretations of the behaviour and institutions we encounter and influence our interactions with others.

Theory is an attempt to organize explanations in a systematic way, to develop a connected and logical understanding of how people and social systems work. To be effective, this search for an overall perspective must be grounded by research that investigates how people actually behave; how they organize their interrelations, their production and their reproduction; and the conditions they face. Such research serves to ensure both that theory helps us understand how things work and that it explains more than the particular kinds of relations and conditions within our immediate and partial view. Although empirical research and theory are integrally interrelated, theory must move beyond the bewildering complexities of individual situations to develop a conception of general patterns and relationships. Theory shapes empirical research, but must also be guided by such research.

To guide our behaviour effectively, theory must be informed by our interaction with our physical and social environment, by our practice. In other words, theory is formulated not simply by formal research, but also according to our daily experience. As we interact with, and change, our world, we can simultaneously modify, challenge, or confirm our theory.

Theory building, then, is a dynamic and ongoing process that cannot easily be separated from research and other forms of action. The tenets of a theory are neither true nor false, but, rather, are more or less useful in understanding the conditions and relations of daily life. This understanding is not simply an intellectual exercise to be performed by a few in-shape academics working out in a seminar room. Explicitly or implicitly, explanations guide what we all do. It is necessary to make theory visible so that we can evaluate its usefulness. Visible, clear, systematic theory is critical to strategies, because we need to know how things currently work in order to change or maintain them and in order to develop an alternative vision.

In providing systematic explanations, theory tells us what to look at, how to look, and what to do about what we find. Nowhere are the connections between theory and subject, method, and practice more obvious than in the study of women and work.

A central feature of the construction of feminist theory has been the exposure of these connections in established theoretical perspectives (see, for example, Eichler, 1975, 1978, 1983; Kealey, 1979; Luxton, 1984; Marsden, 1978, 1981; McCormack, 1979; Prentice, 1978; and Smith, 1975). The purpose in uncovering the male-centred nature of theoretical work has not in the main been to call for theory that would somehow be more objective and value-free. Rather, by making the connections visible, feminist theorists have enabled themselves to more effectively evaluate the usefulness of these approaches. And they have argued convincingly that no theory that fails to encompass women's experience can provide systematic explanations for any social phenomenon.

In developing new theoretical frameworks, feminists have made their own perspectives, and the connections to subject, method, and practice, explicit. They have, to use Dorothy Smith's terms (1977:13-14), taken "the standpoint of women" and "oppose(d) women's oppression." For feminists of all persuasions, "the political goal of equality between the sexes" (Eichler, 1985:622) has been clear. Feminists have differed from other theorists in stating their goals, not in having goals.

Instead of attempting to separate themselves from their subjects, as most social scientists have done, feminist theorists have frequently identified with those whose work they were trying to explain. Feminists' methods have often been explicitly subjective. The famous feminist slogan "the personal is political" has had important theoretical implications. Perhaps most significantly, it has meant that individual female experiences count. Through sharing these experiences, feminist theorists have sought to understand them within the context of larger social structures and processes, to show how these structures and processes shape and are shaped by women's work. The adoption of the tenet that the personal is political has also meant exposing the so-called personal or private problems of family, sexuality, and childbearing and rearing as public issues, which can no longer be hidden in the household.

Subject

It has not been difficult for feminists to establish the connection between theory and subject in relation to work. What has been called work in traditional approaches to theorization is that which is done for pay or profit in the market. Most explanations have focused on waged and salaried workers, owners, and bosses. Unpaid work done in the market has frequently been excluded, as has all unpaid and some paid work done in the home or on the streets.

These exclusions, feminists have pointed out, have meant that the work most women do every day is untheorized. This is not however simply a problem for and of women. It has also meant that traditional theory has failed to develop comprehensive explanations for how work is organized and how it gets done. Unless the kind of labour done mainly by women is integrated into theories of work, the way people survive on a daily basis — the means employed to provide food, clothing, shelter, and care — cannot be understood.

For feminists, theories of work must consider all the labour involved in acquiring what is deemed necessary for survival by different social classes in different racial and cultural groups and in different historical periods. This means including the unpaid labour done for family firms or farms and the volunteer work performed for all manner of organizations and individuals. It means including all unpaid domestic work — the management of the household and its finances, the bearing and rearing of children, the personal services provided for the elderly and for husbands and children of all ages. It also means including the work done for pay in the underground economy — the selling of sex and of typing, cleaning, babysitting, laundry, and sewing services.

Labour force work has certainly been considered by feminist theorists, but in developing their analytical frameworks, they have sought to integrate all forms of labour into their systematic explanation.

Method

The connection between theory and method has been more difficult for feminists to establish. The word "method," as it is used here, refers to the particular way the subject is approached, to both how it is viewed and the assumptions made in developing evidence. Much of traditional theory has started from a male perspective, from what is most real for men. Theories have been based on evidence that was assumed to be value-free, objective, a clear reflection of work as it is. This evidence, however, has often concealed more than it has revealed and has frequently measured only that which has been of concern to men. The issue for feminists, then, has not been simply that women's work should be included, but *how* it should be included.

As some feminists (see, for example, Armstrong and Armstrong, 1983b; Eichler, 1978; Marsden, 1978; and Smith, 1975) have pointed out, many traditional theories of work have assumed at best sexless workers, at worst an all-male cast. Explanations of male employment have often been generalized to apply to all workers. The standard has all too often been male. Sex differences in jobs, in conditions of work, and in the consequences of paid employment have frequently been ignored.

Moreover, labour force work has usually been treated as separate from the household and from other forms of labour. The relationship between men's domestic conditions and their labour force work has remained largely untheorized, because it has been assumed that men's household connections have little impact on their paid jobs.

Not all theoretical frameworks have ignored women's labour or generalized from male work to all work. As Meg Luxton (1984:61) has argued, "in the early period, 'women' were central to social theory but always in the sense described by Simone de Beauvoir as the 'other.'" Explicitly or implicitly, much of traditional theory has assumed that woman's primary attachment is to the home and that this attachment is biologically determined (Sydie,1987). Her labour there has been defined as consumption or leisure, not work. Her connection to the market and to the "public" has been assumed to derive from her connection to her husband. Basic to these approaches have also been the assumptions that women marry, have children, and receive adequate financial support from that primary worker, the male. Male and female "roles" have been taken to be complementary, agreed upon, separate but equal.

When women's paid work has been considered, it has usually been defined as secondary to women and to their employers, as less important than the labour of men. It has also been defined as deviant; as a problem for men, for women, for children, and for employers. Unlike the assumptions made about men's employment, women's labour force work has been linked to their domestic responsibilities. Indeed, women's paid work has largely been understood in terms of their domestic ties, and it has been assumed that this means that they have a choice about taking paid jobs. In traditional theories, as Lorna Marsden (1978:8) has pointed out, "all too often the assumed division of labour is not left problematic." The sexual division of labour, like assumed sex differences in skills, capacities, and attitudes, has been accepted, not questioned.

Feminist theory has challenged the assumptions that most women choose to enter the market, that their work is secondary and that most women have happily or passively accepted their work within and outside of the formal economy. Rather than treat the public and the private as separate for either women or men, feminists have increasingly explained one in terms of the other, making the political personal as well as the personal political. And rather than treat all women as one, feminist theory has increasingly acknowledged differences among women, while also recognizing some shared conditions that unite all women. The sexual division of labour, as well as assumed sex differences in abilities, have become problems, rather than solutions.

The traditional assumptions have been reflected in the methods used to gather the data designed to test and develop theory. The techniques employed in traditional research have not consisted of simply collecting all the facts that require theoretical explanation. Rather, they have entailed the collection of particular facts, facts whose very selection has been influenced by theory. When theory begins by assuming that women are secondary workers whose primary commitment is to home and family, while men are primary breadwinners whose paid employment can be understood in isolation from what happens outside the formal economy, the theorist can see only certain aspects of work. Such theory cannot properly be considered objective, or value-free.

The emphasis on objectivity has been largely responsible for the primacy given to quantitative analysis. Statistical manipulation of numerical evidence has been particularly highly valued as providing the most complete and accurate basis for explanation. But, as feminists have been demonstrating (see, for example, Armstrong and Armstrong, 1982; Benston, 1982; Eichler, 1987; and Gaskell, 1986), this stress on "hard" data has meant that many aspects of labour are left unexplained. What is most easily measured is what gets theorized. Particular characteristics of labour force work are what is easiest to measure.

What is most difficult to translate into numbers that can be statistically analyzed is women's work experiences outside the formal economy, as well as the nature and conditions of work in all areas. The very tools that have been developed in relation to traditional theory have often precluded theoretical consideration of that kind of work and those parts of work which are of crucial importance to women.

Feminist theorists have sought to include women's experiences at work, and perceptions of work, by employing qualitative approaches. They have been skeptical about quantitative data, questioning what is measured by such means. They have been redesigning and combining techniques in an effort to further the understanding of women's work.

Feminists have argued that the first steps in theory construction are the recognition of the link between theory and methods, and a re-examination of these methods. Sex-conscious methods are required; methods that make sex difference a central feature of explanation, and which question, rather than assume, the sexual division of labour.

Practice

Perhaps the most difficult task for feminist theorists has been to establish the link between theory and practice. Systematic explanation, especially in its most abstract and complex form, often appears unrelated to action. It rarely appears to provide much guidance for what is to be done. Yet, by leaving the sexual division of labour unproblematic — by assuming that women's labour in the market is secondary and that their labour in the home merely consumption — traditional theory has been reinforcing existing conditions. The strategy that flows from such theory is conservative, promoting as it does the maintenance of the *status quo*, which frequently leaves women's work invisible and subordinate. In short, such theory provides a justification for the current situation and discourages change.

By contrast, feminist theorists have been committed to change and have been clear about the need to connect theory and strategy. Theory simultaneously grows out of and guides efforts to alter structures. As Mary O'Brien (1981:2) has made clear, "Theory at its best is fundamentally a mode of analyzing human experience which is at the same time a method of organizing that experience." The origins of current theories about women's work can be traced to the turbulent 1960s, when the participation of women in the paid labour force and in post-secondary educational institutions increased dramatically (Armstrong and Armstrong, 1984a:19; Adamson *et al.*, 1988), but the nature and conditions of women's participation remained virtually unchanged. Challenges to authority were widespread but, even within the groups doing the challenging, women were "kept in their place." Women in the Student Union for Peace Action, a Canadian New Left organization, expressed the experience of many women: "One sometimes gets the feeling that we are a civil rights organization with a leadership of southern racists" (Bernstein *et al.*, 1972:38).

It was the activists in the women's movement who, recognizing that the startling growth in women's paid employment has been accompanied by the continued subordination of women, felt most urgently the need to make sense of the position of women and, in particular, of women's work. They focused primarily on work, defined to include both domestic and wage labour, because work is how we provide for most of our daily needs; because work consumes much of our energy; because work has a powerful influence on our health, our relations, our possibilities, and our understanding of the world. Many of the earliest and best contributions were made by movement women and much of their theory espoused a clear commitment to change. Even many who were less actively involved in the women's movement were drawn into confronting inequality and laying the basis for change, once they began to examine women's condition. A shared problem for feminist theorists has been to explain the dramatically increasing involvement of women in the formal economy that is combined with the continuing segregation and subordination of women in all areas of work. Their shared purpose has been to use these explanations as the basis for strategies designed to improve women's condition.

The common commitment to equality, along with the size of the Canadian population, our multicultural heritage, and our colonial experiences, have contributed to what a number of feminists (Armstrong, 1986; Hamilton and Barrett, 1986; Bell, 1987) have described as a peculiarly Canadian characteristic — the extent to which feminists with very different views have talked to each other, learned from each other, marched in the same demonstrations, and taken each other into account. But, although feminists have been united around the goal of equality, there have been significant disagreements about what is meant by equality and therefore about what kind of strategy is useful.

For some, the quest for equality has primarily meant guaranteeing women's individual rights and seeking equality of opportunity. This has entailed the assumption of a male standard and the demand for treatment similar to that of men, the demand for an end to discrimination. For others, the quest for equality has mainly meant improving women's collective rights and seeking equality of condition. This has entailed the demand for not only the recognition of differences, but also fundamental structural change.

These disagreements over the meaning of equality reflect basic disagreements in feminist theoretical perspectives. Although feminists have agreed on the inadequacies of traditional theories and together exposed their links with subject, method, and practice, they have disagreed about how women's work is to be understood. But conflicts among feminists, as well as conflicts between feminists and non-feminists, have contributed to the growing sophistication of theories about women's work, and to new strategies for change.

The Central Questions

The theories expounded in the turbulent 1960s framed many of the questions that remain central to the theorization of women's work. In attempting to expose the fundamental factors involved in establishing the nature and conditions of women's work, these theories often set out stark alternative explanations. Theorists argued about whether women's work is determined mainly by ideas or by material conditions; about whether sex or gender offered the primary explanation for segregated labour; about whether women are passive victims or active initiators; about whether capitalism or patriarchy, production or reproduction, men or women, domestic or wage labour, families or economies, are to blame for women's subordinate position within and outside of the formal economy.

These simplified dichotomies provided, and still provide to some extent, a useful way to begin the analysis of women's work, because they strip bare the confusing complexities of daily life, making more profound theoretical thinking possible. They have sparked heated debate and stimulated a range of empirical studies. The systematic explanations offered by the pioneers have been extended, qualified, altered, and sometimes destroyed by these debates among theorists and by these empirical studies, as well as by changes in women's work. In the process, theory has become more qualified, more dialectical, more sophisticated, and less rigidly oppositional. Explanations have begun to converge as theorists working from a range of perspectives have read, criticized, and responded to each other's work. In the process, feminist theorists have come to some fundamental agreements that have been based both on the obvious inadequacies of some approaches and on clear trends in women's work.

This is not to suggest that most theoretical issues have been neatly resolved, that theoretical debate has ceased, or that most feminist theorists share a common perspective. Indeed, in the following chapters, we argue that the very areas that have provided a basis for convergence remain central to controversies between different perspectives and among those working within a shared theoretical framework. But the debates now take place on the basis of some fundamental agreements and some shared understanding. They are increasingly complex and continue to move in new directions, taking more and more factors into account.

Perspectives on Theory

This book looks at the development, since the 1960s, of various English Canadian explanations of women's work. For several reasons drawn from feminist theory itself, we are not about to present a traditional academic appraisal of English Canadian theorists, which would distance us from the process of theory development. As Dorothy Smith (1974) pointed out in an early and influential contribution to feminist theory, such an approach would reflect the bias of most social science literature, a bias which denigrates the personal, and which claims an objectivity seldom, if ever, realized in fact. Moreover, as feminist theorists have been arguing for two decades now, the connections between the personal and the political must be not only recognized, but made central to any analysis. Finally, for well over a decade we have been researching and writing about women's work. During this time, we have read, criticized, adopted or rejected, but always learned from the theoretical and empirical work of others. To suggest that we could provide an uncommitted presentation of all these contributions would be misleading. It is only by acknowledging and making explicit our own approach that we can contribute to the development of theory. This book, then, presents our perspective on, and our response to, a range of theoretical debates.

While what follows reflects our perspective on theorizing women's work, we certainly would not claim that it is entirely original to us. Indeed, because theoretical developments are related to the changing conditions of women's work — because they alter and are altered by such conditions — our theoretical development reflects what we have learned from various theoretical and empirical contributions. Moreover, it often falls into line with them as we, too, respond to and learn from changes in women's work and in theories about this work.

For several reasons, this book focuses on English Canadian perspectives. The rapid development of theoretical work in recent years means that some selection has been necessary. It is no simple task to sort out English Canadian theory. Such theory has not developed in isolation. Indeed, it has been profoundly influenced by discussions taking place elsewhere, especially in England and the United States, and has played a part in structuring theoretical debates abroad. Moreover, although linguistic and cultural barriers have limited exchanges between English and French Canadian theorists, each group has learned from the other. As Roberta Hamilton and Michèle Barrett (1986:2) have pointed out in the introduction to their book on Canadian feminism, these barriers have meant that theorists ''write from within a political culture built on the recognition rather than the denial of division and difference between people.'' Yet, in spite of all these influences on their thinking, English Canadian theorists have struggled to come to grips with the specificity of women's work experience in English Canada, and have, in the process, developed explanations that are in some ways particular to English Canada.

The cross-fertilization that characterizes Canadian theory has contributed to the move away from simple dichotomies and strictly oppositional stances. So has the extensive research that has allowed the evaluation of theoretical approaches. English Canadian theory, unlike many other approaches, has also been characterized by efforts to combine major theoretical developments with empirical research. Feminists here have worked hard at bridging the gulf between grand theory and abstract empiricism. Such efforts have helped move theorists in similar directions as some approaches are fundamentally challenged, as others are supported by the research, and as new questions arise.

The development of theory is a never-ending and collective process. The very nature of theory building means that no discussion of theory can ever be definitive or comprehensive. What follows is a snapshot of the attempt to construct an understanding of women's work, work that is itself constantly changing. What is presented is a broad overview of perspectives formulated over the last two decades in English Canada to provide systematic explanations of women's work.

Chapter Two

Do Bodies Matter?

Introduction

From the start of the latest wave of feminism, theorists working from a range of perspectives have been united in their rejection of explanations that attributed women's work primarily to biologically determined factors. The segregation of women into a limited number of low-level labour force jobs, and women's responsibility for domestic chores, have long been justified on the basis of women's physical size or shape, their "natural" skills or incapacities, their maternal instincts or emotional makeup, their weakness or strength in bearing children. From this perspective, the existence of the category of women's work is inevitable. In countering such a stance, many feminists have sought to establish scientifically that such differences are in the main socially structured rather than biologically determined at birth. Rejecting biological determinism, they have argued that social conditions can be altered in order to change women's work.

Biological Determinism

Anne-Marie Henshel (1973:27), for example, devoted the first chapter of her book *Sex Structure* to marshalling evidence in support of the argument that "practically all" psychological and aptitudinal differences between women and men "can be explained by cultural factors." The only innate differences, she maintained, are physical ones related to "sexual characteristics, bio-chemistry (hormones), body size, biological vulnerability, and sensory motor" traits.

In *The Double Ghetto*, we wrote a chapter refuting arguments based on biological determinism, concluding that "Some sex differences have biological origins and therefore set limits on human behaviour but even these differences are influenced by the social environment" (Armstrong and Armstrong, 1978:110). As Henshel did in the revised edition of her book (Ambert, 1976:34), we argued that "no simple duality exists, that the opposite sexes are not so opposite" (Armstrong and Armstrong, 1978:98). But, unlike Henshel, we suggested that many of the characteristics associated with each sex may be related to the structure of the work of each as well as to early learning and cultural factors. More recently, Karen Messing (1986:350) has concluded that it is "impossible to prove that differences in mean performance of men and women are the result of biology rather than education and training", and, we would add, working conditions. Segregated employment encourages the development of sex-specific characteristics.

The movement of at least one woman into virtually every labour force occupation made it increasingly difficult for theorists to argue that women were biologically incapable of doing particular kinds of paid work. Women continued to provide primary childcare, however, encouraging the development of both female parenting skills and theories about maternal instinct. In spite of or perhaps because of women's rising labour force participation, many theorists argued that the best childcare is provided by biological mothers, that women need to fulfill themselves through mothering, and that children deprived of such mothers are likely to have social problems. Drawing on research primarily conducted in other countries, we maintained by contrast that there was little "to indicate that biological factors create nurturant or maternal behaviour in human females" (Armstrong and Armstrong, 1978:104). Others, such as Helen Levine and Alma Estable (1981:22), attacked the theory of maternal deprivation, concluding that "there is *no evidence* supporting past claims of the link between delinquency and working mothers." Women, most feminists argued, are not born with particular skills that predetermine their work in or out of the household. The purpose of this feminist research was to convince both women and men that work divisions were socially structured, not biologically determined.

To some extent, radical feminists were an exception in rejecting biology as an explanation. American Shulamith Firestone (1970:9), in presenting what still stands up as a cogent and articulate statement of radical feminism, argued that "the natural reproductive difference between the sexes led directly to the first division of labor at the origins of class.'' She went on to assert that fundamental equality can be achieved only when the technological means for eliminating sex differences are developed and utilized. In her view, women must cease to gestate, menstruate, and lactate in order to participate on the same basis as men. Canadian radical feminists such as Bonnie Kreps (1972:74-75) explicitly identified with Firestone's framework and located women's oppression in male control of women's bodies, but seemed to distance themselves somewhat from the biological arguments by stressing sex roles and ascribed characteristics. Technological means of making women like men were seldom discussed.

The Sex/Gender Distinction

Increasingly, feminist theorists used the term "gender" to label the socially constructed differences between women and men and to draw attention to the nonbiological origins of women's position. According to Marlene Mackie, in the introduction to her book *Exploring Gender Relations* (1983:1), "Sex is the biological dichotomy between females and males. It is determined at conception and is, for the most part, unalterable. Gender, on the other hand, is what is socially recognized as femininity and masculinity." From this perspective, gender, not sex, is the major factor explaining women's work.

The use of the distinction between sex and gender has become widespread as efforts to combat assumptions about the biologically determined work and characteristics of women and men continue. It is important, especially in the face of the growing appeal of sociobiology, to counter the claims that maternal instinct and children's dependency inextricably tie women and children to each other and to men within heterosexual monogamous marriages, and that innate female characteristics provide a decisive basis for slotting women into particular kinds of work and for excluding them from others. Without such theory, strategies for change would need to resort to plans for altering human biology.

But, as we have argued (Armstrong and Armstrong, 1984b:184), it is very difficult to distinguish the socially assigned from the biologically determined. Is menstruation simply a biological process, or is it an experience that can be altered, even in its measurable physical manifestations, by social conditions and relations? And how can we explain the cultural variability in the physical experience of childbirth if we categorize it as exclusively biologically determined? To use the term "gender" is, at least in certain circumstances, to make the unwarranted suggestion that the distinction is clearly established.

Even if sex-specific biological characteristics can be clearly separated from socially assigned ones, the characteristics themselves still have meaning only within the context of class, race and history. And they are still influenced by the economic environment and by the available technology. For example, although the male tendency to have a slightly greater muscle mass than that of women may make some of the work of men engaged in physical toil more valuable in a society dependent on brute human strength, the worth of this labour alters significantly in societies or classes where it is intellectual skill that is primarily required or where physical power comes from machines. There are also significant differences between the value attached to the childbearing capacities of paupers and those of queens, and between those of white women and those of Native women.

Furthermore, to speak of "gender" is to imply, inaccurately, that biology is outside society and history; that it is, in Mackie's terms, unalterable. We know that pregnancy today has different physical and social consequences for women than it did a century ago, and that the physical aspects of pregnancy differ not only according to whether women live in Ethiopia or Canada, but also according to whether they are rich or poor Canadians. Poor women, for instance, are more likely to miscarry. Native women are much more likely than other Canadian women to die in childbirth. And young Canadian women today tend to start menstruating at an earlier age than did the young women of several generations ago. Biological structures, as well as the evaluation and implications of such structures, vary with privilege and over time, but an emphasis on gender suggests that biology need not — indeed, cannot — be theorized.

Finally, gender is increasingly losing its usefulness as a means of distinguishing between learned behaviour and biologically determined differences as the term is increasingly used to refer to all differences between women and men. Job applications ask about gender even though employers simply want to know whether the applicant is female or male, not whether she or he is feminine or masculine. Enrolment figures claim to provide data on the gender of students, although it is difficult to see how information on behaviour patterns was collected. It would be more useful to return to the term "sex" and to focus on the social conditions that shape all aspects of people's lives, rather than to suggest that biology can be isolated, or to make a show of non-sexism by referring to gender.

Biology Reconsidered

Once it had been empirically established by feminist researchers that women's subordination is in the main socially constructed, it became possible to reassess the somewhat dangerous topic of the significance of women's reproductive capacities.

The early arguments for bringing biology back in often came from those who supported a dual systems approach. From this perspective, the system of capitalism gives rise to class inequalities created largely in the market. The system of patriarchy (a term generally used to mean male dominance), centred on the home and the reproduction of children, engenders the specific oppression of women. Although these systems are seen to interact, sometimes reinforcing and sometimes contradicting each other, they remain separate. Each has its own logic and history. These theorists argued that, although marxism may expose the workings of capitalism, feminist analytical tools are required in order to reveal the foundations of patriarchy. Understanding patriarchy means understanding women's unique physiological aspects, especially their ability to bear children.

In setting out her dual systems argument, and addressing what she considered the limits of marxism, Roberta Hamilton (1978:85) held that "inherent in the biological differences is an inequality which human society can struggle to overcome but which a theoretical treatment of the situation of women can scarcely ignore." Writing from a radical feminist perspective, Mary O'Brien (1979:104) took up a similar theme in "Reproducing Marxist Man," pointing out that "birth is not an object of philosophy — Marxist man, impressively human as he is, somehow never gets born." Moreover, as some other theorists maintained, a gender focus not only ignored biology but also often resulted in efforts to prove that "women were capable of being the same as men" (Miles, 1982:215). Instead of stressing similarities between females and males they argued for an emphasis on the specificity of women and on a recovery of motherhood. Angela Miles (1982:216), for example, claimed that "only a feminism that recognizes and affirms women's specificity can develop the alternative rationality required for the principle of Totality and the move beyond sectional pressure to a universal challenge to society."

The specificity of women's reproductive capacities also lies at the heart of the complex theoretical argument developed by Mary O'Brien (1981) in *The Politics of Reproduction*. Like the earlier work of Firestone, this text stands out as an articulate, perceptive, and sophisticated explanation of women's continuing subordination. For O'Brien (1981:44),

Our feminist perspective is a maternal perspective, in that it attempts to root this long oppression in material biological process, rather than in mute, brute biology.

Men experience reproduction mainly as the alienation of their male seed, and this, it is argued, motivates them to seek control over both mother and child. "Men claim more than the child; they claim ownership of the woman's reproductive labour power in a sense recognizably similar to, but by no means analogous with, the sense in which capitalists appropriate the surplus labour power of wage labourers" (58). Women and men cannot have the same experiences; they cannot be the same.

The arguments of Hamilton and O'Brien convinced many feminists that any theoretical framework that could not take biological factors into account is inadequate; that biological differences have to be recognized and theorized, not ignored. O'Brien's contention that women's specific participation in reproduction is a key factor in their oppression was difficult to refute. Moreover, O'Brien's theory of reproduction, like Marx's theory of capitalist production, did offer a motivating force. In O'Brien's theory, the alienation of the male seed was put forth as the driving energy behind men's domination of women.

This did not, however, provide an explanation of women's subordination that had anything like the power of Marx's analysis of free wage labour. Marx's theory explained how the drive to accumulate reduces and often eliminates alternative means of survival, with the result that more and more people have to sell their ability to work in return for a wage. Meanwhile, capitalists have little choice about seeking to increase surplus value, to seek higher and higher profits. Otherwise, competition will eliminate them as well. Both competition and the struggle between owners and workers create change.

In O'Brien's theory, it was not clear why men would be increasingly compelled to control women, or why women would have few alternatives to submission until new technology developed. Whereas the drive to accumulate offered an explanation of change, the alienation of the male seed did not. It is necessarily a static notion, at least for long periods of history. Conquest merely has to be maintained, but profits must increase. Although O'Brien (21) argued that the process changed historically, she maintained that there were only two periods of "significant historical change" in reproduction: "the historical discovery of physiological paternity" and "the much more recent change in reproduction praxis." And she did not make clear how or why these came about.

Furthermore, Marx's analysis of production held out the prospects of contradictions creating the possibility for different futures, and of people's active participation in the making of their own history. For Marx, the search for profit creates the conditions for revolution. It is difficult to see from O'Brien's analysis why women are becoming active in demanding change, given their historical submission and the continuing alienation of the male seed. For O'Brien (63), the "Age of Contraception" offers the technical means for the transformation of the social relations of reproduction, but she did not provide an adequate explanation of how or why these means develop. In Marx's theory, technological change is understood primarily in terms of owners' efforts to reduce labour costs and increase control over the labour process. The technology mainly serves to enhance the owners' power. An expanded theory of reproduction technology would have to consider why these technologies develop and how they may actually serve to limit the possibilities for women's control over contraception and birth. O'Brien began such an analysis, but the process of change remained obscure. Finally, the articulation of the systems of production and reproduction and the nature of their relationship over time, as well as the logic of the reproductive system itself, remained unclear (at least, to us) within O'Brien's framework.

Bodies in History

Stimulated by O'Brien to tackle some of the problems raised in and by her analysis, we argued in "Beyond Sexless Class and Classless Sex: Towards Feminist Marxism" (Armstrong and Armstrong, 1983b: see especially 27-28) that biological differences take on a particular significance under the capitalist mode of production. A defining characteristic of capitalism is free wage labour. The sale and purchase of the peculiar commodity that marxists term "labour power" (or the capacity to labour) seemed to us to entail the reproduction of free wage labourers to a certain extent *outside* the capitalist production process proper. To be free in this sense requires some time spent in activities other than paid work and some ability to move from employer to employer. In other words, free wage labour necessarily involves some separation of a public, commodity-production unit from an apparently private subsistence sphere. To be free, workers must be reproduced outside the direct control of individual capitalists. Some aspects of having and nurturing children must occur under conditions different from those found in the market. If produced directly under capitalist conditions, children would of necessity themselves become commodities, and thus could not become free wage labourers (selling their own labour power as a commodity). Moreover, the ideologies of the free wage labourer and of individual rights would be difficult to maintain. Just how children are brought up outside the market varies from society to society and with the efforts of people to shape their own lives and those of their children. Yet the paradoxical fact remains that for capitalism, with its free wage labourers, to endure, capital must not get deeply involved in one particular business, that of raising children. This is not to suggest that the sexual division of labour and the subordination of women appeared with or exist only under capitalism. "Money, class differences, the sexual division of labour — they all predate capitalism, but all acquire a different significance and form under this mode" (Armstrong and Armstrong, 1983:12).

Given this non-capitalist raising of children and given women's unique childbearing capacities, mothers are, at least temporarily, less able than men to participate fully in the labour force. Male and female workers are not interchangeable because the labour of having children cannot be completely equalized under capitalism. What counts in capitalism is money, and many women are somewhat less able than men to participate in the market sphere where money is made, and where the commodities that are valued to the point of being fetishized are produced. In a market where employers are constantly seeking to increase surplus value, the interruptions in women's employment patterns offer a basis for dividing workers and reducing employment costs while ensuring the reproduction of the next generation of employees. The extent to which employees are successful in doing this will depend on women's and men's efforts to determine their own lives.

The particular duties associated with procreation are matters of history, but the sexual division of labour itself is integral to capitalism, providing the material basis for inequality between the sexes. It is free wage labour, not the division of labour by sex or the separation of the public and private spheres, that is the defining characteristic of capitalism, but this characteristic permits segregation both within and outside of the market. It is no accident of history that the everyday tasks of maintaining and reproducing workers for the market have in fact been disproportionately performed by women and have provided the basis for the elaboration of sex differences in the market as well. Nor is it any accident of history that women's domestic and childbearing work is less valued than their paid employment. Thus, in our view, it is the capitalist mode of production, and not biology *per se*, that renders women subordinate and ensures that their reproductive capacities are a liability rather than a resource. Biological capacities are structured, defined, and evaluated within the political economy.

We argued not only that the combination of women's reproductive capacities and the necessity of free wage labour to capitalism provided the basis for their subordination while allowing for wide variations in the form of that subordination, but also that biological characteristics are not fixed. Bodies, too, have histories. Canadians today grow taller than their ancestors, women menstruate at an earlier age, and childbirth is often an easier, less life-threatening process. Economic conditions, including the kinds of work women must do, the kinds of food available, sanitary facilities, housing, and the need for child labour, all influence women's physical structure, their sexual experiences, their pregnancies, and their chances of survival. Technological innovations that are part of capitalist development help structure birth control, childbirth, health care, food distribution, and working conditions; factors which in turn influence women's physical possibilities. State policies and regulations establish conditions for paid work, for birth control and abortion, for standards of health and safety, for participation in sexual relationships and marriage.

If they are considered at all, these material conditions are often explained as manifestations of modernization, urbanization, industrialization, and individual invention, which are considered to progressively lead to a better life for all. Yet changes in the production system do not automatically improve conditions for women and many of these changes have contradictory effects. For instance, the new reproductive technology, which has increased women's chances for surviving childbirth, has also reduced women's control over birthing and denigrated their knowledge while dehumanizing the experience and placing it largely under male direction. Women have free choice in marrying and bearing children but, like the free wage labourers who have no alternative to selling their labour power, women are freely compelled by the conditions of pregnancy, wage work, medical techniques, the dominant ideology, and legal restrictions to marry and have babies in particular ways.

Moreover, changes result mainly from the search for profit rather than from any desire to improve women's condition or from some inevitable drive towards progress. Declining fertility rates, for instance, partially reflect women's growing need to acquire wages through work in the labour market. And women's lower wage rates serve to increase profits and to encourage women to marry men.

The history of bodies, then, is not smooth and linear. It is dialectical and contradictory. Moreover, it also reflects struggles. Women have not been mere vessels, waiting to nurture the male seed. Women have seldom passively accepted the dictates of the church, of the state, of men, or of their bodies (see McLaren, 1984). The contradiction between the technical possibility of women controlling their bodies and the lack of control that results from policies designed for other interests has formed a basis of women's protests for centuries. In their study of contraception and abortion in Canada, Angus McLaren and Arlene Tigar McLaren (1986:30) concluded that "women, though often assumed to be passive in relation to their fertility, went to great lengths in order to control it."

Furthermore, childbearing and sexual relations have been used by women throughout history as a means of resistance against imposed standards and against the more powerful. Meg Luxton's study of Flin Flon families has demonstrated how women have used their bodies to extend choices or escape restrictions. Pregnancy has offered a means of leaving parental homes and sex a way of acquiring "something for the house" (Luxton, 1980:64). Not incidently, Luxton's research has revealed how conditions in the market influence both sexual relations and the form of women's resistance.

Women's bodies and women's desire to control the implications of their physiology have provided a basis for shared concerns and for organized opposition. However, the variation created by existing material conditions has encouraged women in different classes, in different marital situations, and in different racial or ethnic groups to experience their bodies in different ways, and have thus caused divisions among women. Women differ in terms of the health care they receive during pregnancy; in terms of their access to information on birth control and on the ways their bodies function; in terms of ease of gestation as it is related to nutrition, information, and exercise; and in terms of the possibility of escape from repeated pregnancies or violent marriages. They also differ in terms of the consequences of childbearing. The degree of financial and emotional stress created by the birth of children and the limitations children impose on women's movement and participation structure not only women's choices but also the physiological experience of giving birth. Childbirth for Mila Mulroney cannot be the same as it is for a lone welfare mother who already has three hungry children. Of course, dominant (and less dominant) ideologies have also played a role. The debates over birth control and abortion provide just one example of how women's experiences of birth and women's prospects for pregnancy are influenced by ideas about both physiology and human rights (see Jenson, 1986).

In sum, we argued that marxist analytical tools should be used to examine biological factors; that bodies should be understood from a perspective that is historical, materialist, and dialectical. This involves the recognition of difference together with a rejection of the notion that difference necessarily means inequality. Unlike those who argued that biological differences must be eliminated because they create inequality, we argued that the political economic system made biological differences a basis for women's subordination. It is this system, not bodies, that requires transformation.

There is, however, no guarantee that inequality will disappear with capitalism's demise. Unless women and men take both biological and political economic conditions into account, no alternative egalitarian system can be devised. Unlike those who viewed women as having bodies that were unchanged throughout history, we argued that political and economic conditions altered bodies and dictate the ways in which women of different classes experienced their bodies in different ways. Rather than simply providing a basis for subordination, bodies also offered a means and impetus for women's resistance and for some access to power. Unlike those who favoured a dual systems approach, we argued that there was a single system, dominated by the drive to accumulate but shaped by contradictions and people's efforts to structure their own lives. We argued for a historical, materialist analysis of women's bodies, but such an analysis still remains to be developed.

Our argument, as Patricia Connelly (private communication) has pointed out, rests on the assumption that the labour of pregnancy and birth cannot be equalized under capitalism, that it could not be done the same way by women and by men. But new technological innovations do produce a vision of just this possibility. Babies could be produced with ova and sperm extracted from donors and developed in an artificial womb. Capitalist firms could conceivably produce the commodity of labour power under market conditions, virtually eliminating women's specific involvement. But were workers to be produced in this way, they would no longer be *free* wage labourers. The production of workers in the market would mean that they no longer had time away from market conditions and therefore they would no longer be free to move from employer to employer. The private production of workers would also tend towards monopoly, further limiting the possibility of free wage labour. If workers were produced instead by the state, it would be equally difficult to maintain free wage labour, and the required expansion of the state would itself threaten the existence of capitalism. Nonetheless, the technological developments surrounding the reproduction of people cry out for theorization. For example, there is no reason for the demise of capitalism to necessitate the end of women's subordination, especially if it were to involve the complete male appropriation of women's unique capacities.

Connelly has not been alone in her objections to our argument. In her article "Gender and Reproduction, or Babies and the State," Jane Jenson (1986:25) maintained that "by correctly identifying the interpretation of biology as a social construct," we are "left with no argument for why biological differences will necessarily lead to inferiority for those who bear children. Inferiority can only be historically determined." We would certainly agree. Indeed, we argued that biology does not necessarily lead to inferiority and that inferiority is historically determined. We also agree that "gender relations cannot be reduced to material conditions" (Jenson, 1986:24). But we contend that the very pervasiveness of male power indicates that sex differences cannot be equated, as Jenson suggests, with inequities related to race and language. Biological factors, as O'Brien (1981) has made clear, are part of our material conditions. Clearly, however, we are far from an adequate theory of biology and women's varying positions throughout history.

Mothering

An important issue raised but not clarified by these debates has been that of the relationship of women to children. Early theorists, ourselves included (Armstrong and Armstrong, 1978), stressed that women need not be mothers and children need not be cared for by their mothers. Motherhood is nonetheless seldom a real choice. The high cost and scarcity of convenient, good childcare, the structure of labour force jobs, women's low wages, the limited nature of maternity leave, and the absence of paternity leave all mean that women have few alternatives to mothering. Without real choices and without much assistance or social support, mothering can be oppressive for both parent and child (see Levine and Estable, 1981). Sensitive to its many negative aspects, feminists have frequently advocated severe limits on motherhood, either through the rejection of childbirth altogether or through the reallocation of the work to men or to childcare centres.

Such an emphasis was probably necessary in order to counter the powerful ideology of motherhood, but it failed to provide a theory of women's relationship to children. Meg Luxton's (1980:80-115) research on Flin Flon households offered important insights into the contradictory nature of motherhood, an experience that is simultaneously joyful and painful. More theoretical work is needed, however, especially as more and more women are prevented by labour force responsibilities from spending long hours with their children, and many find that alternative arrangements provide little if any improvement on traditional practices. As feminists have babies, efforts to develop a more adequate understanding of motherhood increase.

How women can love and relate to children without sentencing themselves to a secondary position in our society, and indeed whether they can, remains a central issue for feminist theory and practice. As Heather Jon Maroney (1985:44) points out in her review of the literature on motherhood,

> Here the women's movement walks a tightrope strung between offensive and defensive poles: it must assert feminist theory in our own terms, validating "what women do" (and have done historically) in mothering at the same time as it contests patriarchal glorification of the role at the expense of the occupant.

No longer prepared to argue that women are really the same as men, feminists have not developed a theoretical or strategic understanding of difference. Nor have class, race, and ethnic differences in mothering received much theoretical or empirical attention.

Technologies and Reproductive Work

The rapidly changing reproductive technologies are bringing a certain urgency to the theoretical questions related to mothering. Technologies are expanding enormously the ability to manipulate procreation. Contraception and abortion techniques permit greater control over conception. Surrogate mothering, artificial insemination, embryo transfer, and *invitro* fertilization allow new possibilities for conception and gestation. Genetic engineering and prenatal screening techniques offer choices about the kinds of children that are born, who they are born to, what traits and sex they carry, and how the pregnancy happens. They thus raise crucial issues concerning women's right and responsibility to bear and rear children. Indeed, most of the fundamental questions related to women's work in general are brought sharply into focus by technologies that are profoundly altering the conditions and relations of women's childbearing work.

Reproductive technologies have been proliferating during a period of steady growth in female labour-force participation and of continuing decline in female fertility. To some (see, for example, Romaniuc, 1984), the coincidence of these patterns indicate women's increasingly successful demand for control over their bodies, their growing independence, and their expanding choices. Moreover, the reproductive technologies seem to hold out the possibility of eliminating what Firestone (1970) argued were restrictions imposed on women by their reproductive capacities. With biological differences reduced or wiped out, women and men would finally be equal.

But these technologies have been developing during a period when more and more aspects of human activity, especially of women's activities, are coming under medical and state control. For many feminist theorists (see, for example, Bercovitch, 1986; Brodribb, 1986; Coffey, 1986; Lippman, 1986; Overall, 1986, 1987; and Rogers, 1986), the very nature of these technologies reflect what Mary O'Brien (1981) argued was the male desire to control women's reproductive capacities. The way these technologies are being developed and used means that other people — mainly the men who own the companies that produce the technologies and support the research, the men who direct hospitals, and the doctors who prescribe and treat (as well as the predominately male legislators who establish the regulations) — increasingly have control over individual women's bodies and the conception, gestation, and delivery of children. In accordance with state legislation, doctors decide which Canadian women can have access to the most effective means of birth control; which are eligible for fertility drugs, *invitro* fertilization, and prenatal screening. Doctors and legislators, some feminists (see, for example, Brodribb, 1986; Coffey, 1986; and Tait, 1986) maintain, may use legislation on the new technologies to reinstate male power over female sexuality, limiting access to "healthy" women in regularized, heterosexual unions, and increasing control over children. Although the technologies extend the capacity to manipulate human reproduction, they also make it possible to treat women more, rather than less, like biological machines, as the stories collected by Rehner (1989) suggest.

Surrogate motherhood is just one example of the reduction of women to their reproductive capacities and the potential for transferring control to others. A woman who agrees to carry a baby for another is in effect renting out her body for close to a year, during which others have a say in her sexual relationships, her diet, her social and economic activities. As Somer Brodribb (1986:418) has pointed out, although individual women can refuse to be surrogates, many women's inferior economic and social conditions restrict the alternatives available to them and encourage them to take on what has been referred to as a new form of prostitution. The production of children is becoming more a market and legal process, governed by laws and technologies that are unlikely, given current conditions, to make women more equal to men. Indeed, these developments may reduce women's control over what has sometimes been a source of strength as well as a limiting process: the conception, gestation and birthing of a child.

Furthermore, these reproductive technologies may serve to increase differences among women. Those with financial resources and heterosexual partners may have greater access to techniques designed to promote conception and manipulate pregnancy than do women who are poor, disabled, or lesbian. Those with few financial resources may have little choice about bearing children for women who are more financially secure and have other priorities. Although some individual women's control may be increased, women's collective rights may be diminished.

Reproductive technologies highlight the contradictory nature of increasing control over procreation. They also suggest that we can no longer think in terms of the simple alternatives of either eliminating or maintaining biological differences. They demonstrate how much biologies and technologies are influenced by — indeed cannot be separated from — economic and social conditions, as well as ideology. They also emphasize our need to theorize women's childbearing work — to understand the complicated conditions and relations of a job that may no longer be uniquely female.

Conclusion

The theoretical debates about biology have in a way come full circle, although current discussions are much more complex and, at the same time, share some common tenets. The convergence centres on the social construction of women's subordination. Few, if any, feminists would now argue that women have innate biological characteristics that inevitably determine their work, or their subordination. And few Canadian feminists would argue that men's biological makeup drives them to subordinate women. As Mariana Valverde (1985:15) has explained in *Sex, Power and Pleasure*, attributing male aggression to biology

> confuses men's social power — which is what gives the penis its threatening meaning — with physiological facts. Physiology does not in itself allow men to perform the complex social act of rape: it is rather a patriarchal social system which permits men to abuse women in various ways including rape.

This convergence of the social construction of both female and male actions has allowed for the development of new concerns. ''Differences of race, class, and sexual practice have become a primary focus of theoretical discussion'' (Code, 1988:21).

Meanwhile, there has been a move to integrate women's specific reproductive capacities into theoretical frameworks. This tendency has permitted theorists to avoid the use of a male standard — to avoid the pressure to argue that women can be just like men — opening up a range of possible alternative explanations for human characteristics and for the structure of work. However, it has also created new issues for debate.

For some, it has meant the celebration of specific female traits and capacities; for others, a reexamination of the historically specific uses, evaluations, and transformations of reproductive capacities. In this context, the adoption of the concept of "gender" a decade or more ago is understandable, as feminists were defensively, yet properly, insisting that some if not most aspects of women's subordination were socially constructed. At a time when new reproductive technologies lend urgency to such feminist explorations, however, it seems to us appropriate for feminists to go on the offensive, to reject a stark distinction between sex and gender while exploring the socially constructed aspects of human biology itself. As Mary O'Brien (1987:6) makes clear,

the immense expansion of the possibility of male control of women's fertility, or the abolition of women in the creation of a technological womb, is such that we have to think of a politics of reproduction. We must also abandon the notion of childbearing as "essentially" biological. It has, in fact, never been that.

Chapter Three

What About Ideas?

Introduction

Rejecting arguments that attributed the segregation and subordination of women's work primarily to biology, many feminist theorists looked instead to ideas for explanations of women's work. For such theorists as those we categorized as idealist (Armstrong and Armstrong, 1978:111-132), women's work can essentially be understood in terms of shared belief systems and appropriate behaviour patterns associated with the female and male roles children learn to play. This belief system is manifested both in attitudes employers hold about female workers and in the choices women are assumed to make about when and where they work.

Although other theorists have challenged the primacy and independence given to ideas by these feminist theorists, they have not denied either that ideas are important in our explanations of women's work or that ideas should be theoretically understood. Both radical feminists and socialist feminists have argued however that ideas cannot be explained in isolation from the work women do or from structures of power. Radical feminists have tended to relate ideas to women's reproductive labour and to patriarchal ideology, while socialist feminists have emphasized the need to place ideology within the context of a political economy dominated by some men and by the search for profit.

The continuing debate, then, has not been about whether ideas are important, but rather about how important ideas are in explaining women's work. Equally significant has been the question of how ideas are to be understood. How do they develop; how do they change; how do they differ — not only for women and for men, but also among women?

Cultural Determinism

Especially for those trained in the functionalist perspective, an approach particularly common in the social sciences in the United States, culture seemed to provide a more attractive and rational explanation for women's work than did biology. From this perspective, cultures — not biology — are seen to have assigned different tasks to males and females. Characterized by common belief systems, cultures determine the behaviour pattern known as a role (see Eichler, 1980:12) and create expectations about suitable work for women.

From birth, children are socialized into roles that are different for each sex and that are differently valued by each sex. Learning roles means learning sex-specific beliefs and behaviour patterns. Such early learning provides the foundation for later years, but some adult socialization and resocialization continues throughout life.

As psychologist Esther Greenglass (1973: 110) explained in an early article, "Intensive differential socialization programmes for male and female result in members of the two sexes seeking and valuing quite different experiences and attributes within themselves." Similarly, the Report of the Royal Commission on the Status of Women (Canada, 1970:20) argued that "Sex roles established in the family have followed women and men into the economic world" where "lack of recognition of women's potential" helps keep women doing women's work.

There are various theories about how socialization takes place and about the relative influence of role models, selective sanctions, and cognitive development (see Greenglass, 1982:Chapter 3; Mackie, 1983:Chapters 4, 5, and 6). Nevertheless, most theorists using this approach agree that families, schools, books, toys, and media images play crucial parts in developing ideas internalized in childhood and in reinforcing these ideas throughout the adult years (see Robinson and Salamon, 1987). These ideas and roles guide both women and men into sex-appropriate work within and outside of the household. They also encourage employers to give preference to one sex for particular kinds of work. According to Greenglass's *A World of Difference: Gender Roles in Perspective* (1982:192), the "persistent difference in the employment of men and women, both in status and in kind, represents the culmination of the roles that society has prepared them to enact.''

Like functionalist theorists, symbolic interactionists have also focused on roles and meanings in order to explain women's work. Symbolic interactionists, however, have tended to depend less on the assumption that roles are assigned by a society united in a common belief system, and more on meanings and roles that are understood to be a result of social interaction. From this perspective, women and men are active protagonists in negotiating meanings rather than passive recipients of cultural beliefs. According to Jack Haas and William Shaffir (1978:48), sex role behaviour becomes ''scripted'' behaviour. This behaviour is played out in accordance with ''culturally produced sets of meanings'' that devalue women and their work (Mackie, 1987:28).

This does not mean, Marlene Mackie (1987:192) argued in *Constructing Women and Men*, that symbolic interactionists rely on ideas alone to explain women's segregation and subordination. ''Rather, symbols and social structure are interdependent.'' Nevertheless, analysis begins with social interaction that ''proceeds by means of symbols,'' and ideas are at the core of the role concept that is central to this theoretical perspective.

Approaches that focus on ideas and roles have provided the theoretical basis for a wide range of empirical investigations designed to establish differences in the ways male and female children are socialized, in the images of females and males presented in the media, and in the ideas held by members of each sex about themselves and each other. A variety of research studies have indicated that many women and men have different attitudes about and perceptions of their work (see, for example, Andersen, 1972; Boyd, 1975), that male and female children are often treated in different ways (see, for example, Pike and Zureik, 1975; Russell, 1978), that the males and females portrayed in the media usually have sex-specific characteristics and occupations (see, for example, the Canadian Advisory Committee on the Status of Women, 1978; Pyke and Stewart, 1974), and that women's and men's work is frequently differently valued (see, for example, Cook, 1976; Eichler, 1977; and Ostry, 1968).

Such research seems to support a theory that explains segregation in terms of the parts children learn to play in the theatre of life and in terms of the attitudes members of both sexes acquire about appropriate male and female behaviour. Stereotypes of what women and men can and should do seem to offer an explanation that also provides a solution. Change the stereotypes and women's opportunities will be altered. Change the role models, the sanctions, the toys, and the media images, and women's work will be transformed. The description of roles seems so sensible, so reflective of daily life experience, that the implications and explanatory power of role theory and of analysis based on ideas have seldom been critically examined.

Indeed, because the term "role" offers such a neat and simple way of emphasizing the social construction of inequality, it has been used by a wide range of theorists. And because the concept is so easy to grasp, because it seems so sensible, because it offers attainable solutions that do not involve fundamental changes either in bodies or in social structures, research based on role theory has provided the impetus for a range of policy changes in the fields of media and education. The importance of these changes should not be underestimated. But it is precisely because the term "role" has come to be so widely used that it is important to explore the limitations of its explanatory power.

Roles and the Division of Labour by Sex

Notwithstanding its centrality to the theoretical perspectives that begin with ideas, role theory is more descriptive than analytical, as Margrit Eichler (1980:11) has pointed out in *The Double Standard*. When feminists tried to use the concept of role as a major part of the explanation for the division of labour by sex, a number of fundamental problems emerged.

First, there is the difficulty of explaining how roles develop. For most functionalist theorists, roles are assigned by an overarching society or culture that seems to stand above individuals and organizations. A gender role "includes the prescribed behaviours, attitudes and characteristics associated with gender status" (Greenglass, 1982:10) and the prescription is drawn up by culture. Society becomes an entity that does things to people; an abstraction that is the cause rather than the location of human behaviour. This personification of society suggests processes that are beyond human control and diverts attention from the interests served, from people's ability to shape their lives, and from the structural supports for the division of labour by sex. In the end, the explanation for roles is that culture made them, but it is not clear how or why, or even how this culture is constituted. It is therefore difficult to develop strategies designed to create new patterns of behaviour and new expectations.

For symbolic interactionists, roles do not result solely from a shared meaning system. They also emerge from negotiations. Thus, these theorists have offered some explanation for the development of roles. But why women so consistently lose in these negotiations, and why their work is culturally devalued, is not explained. Nor is there any explanation for the setting of the setting, of the relationships between different sets of negotiations. Why should the scripts in all these various theatres of life emerge with similar characters, with women doing women's work at women's wages? Within this theoretical framework, there are few clues to help us understand the limits imposed on most women's choices or the social structures that help shape individual lives. Again, ideas are the problem in the end, but the emergence of a dominant ideology that consistently relegates women to a secondary place is not explained.

From the earliest years, many of the feminists who began by using role and functionalist theory moved away from an approach that understood societies as being based on a shared belief system and instead started to think in terms of a patriarchal ideology. This has generally meant rejecting a concept of a neutral set of beliefs uniting society and assuming, instead, a system of ideas that justified male power and that were imposed on women by men. These feminists were rejecting the notion, central to most functional theory, that a shared value system was equally beneficial to all. Patriarchal ideology, rather than society, became the agency assigning roles. But, like society, patriarchal ideology frequently became an abstraction that did things to people. There has been little systematic explanation of how or why patriarchal ideology developed or of why men, not women, were able to determine the system of beliefs. Moreover, it was not clear why women had not worked together to alter these ideas imposed by men.

In symbolic interaction theory, the concept of male power has been added to help overcome the problem of explaining the subordination of female roles. According to Mackie (1987:28), males, like the members of other dominant groups, "propagated definitions of the situation that aggrandized themselves and their work." Women, like the members of other subordinate groups, accepted "the dominant groups' definitions." Mackie's (62-63) explanation of why women comply with this ideology has expanded on the tenets of symbolic interaction theory. She has suggested that there are five factors responsible for what she calls women's false consciousness: women's acceptance of social control myths, the "right wing, authoritarian backlash," social control mechanisms, women's traditional ties to men combined with their isolation from other women, and, finally, the fact that some women benefit from the current situation. The last two factors stress social structures rather than ideology, indicating, as Mackie (64) points out, the need to understand "the interaction of ideas and material conditions." In other words, solving the problem of role inequality means moving away from theories that focus primarily on ideas and roles to explain women's place, although it does not mean abandoning the effort to explain how and why ideas develop, or ignoring their impact.

The second major difficulty with theories that rely primarily on roles and ideas concerns the explanation of change. For those using a functionalist approach, children and adults are socialized in a passive, undialectical manner. The implication is a one-way adjustment, an unresisting and uncritical acceptance of appropriate behaviour. There is little room or reason for collective action or even for individual choice. Attitudes, behaviours, and occupations follow more or less automatically from these learned roles. The real problem, then, is not to explain why most women do women's work at women's wages, but why some women don't.

This is not to suggest that those who use role theory have ignored change. Indeed, because roles are understood to be adopted at least in part through imitation, these theorists have focused on altering the images of women. The portrayals of women on television, in books, and in movies, the toys children play with, and the practices of parents have been attacked because they socialize individuals into traditional roles. Similarly, affirmative action has frequently been promoted on the grounds that women who enter fields dominated by men will provide models for other women to emulate.

Change is also understood to result from rational argument. A second strategy to alter roles has been the exposure of unfairness, or of the variable behaviour that denies stereotypes. Because unequal roles are assumed to result from learning sex-specific behaviour or from false ideas about women's capabilities, efforts have been directed towards making people aware of the problem and encouraging them to change their minds.

As feminists developed strategies for change based on role theory, the limitations of the theory became increasingly evident. Efforts to change the roles children played in games, the images in texts and on television, and the models provided by people in power were certainly aided by an exposure of inequity and by demonstrations of women's capacities. But even those strategies designed primarily to alter images, "stereotypes," and expectations required much more than the presentation of ideas considered more appropriate or the exposure of the gap between myth and reality. Teachers, employers, and media managers resisted, not only because the alternatives contradicted their beliefs but also because they had something to lose, at least in the short run. Moreover, the role models, the book content, and the nature of games could not be changed without changing structures and introducing policies that made it necessary for people to alter their practices. Ideas were not enough.

Feminists had problems with using role theory both because it has limited explanatory power and because, to the extent that it did offer explanations, it mainly served to justify the current situation. It was therefore difficult to use in challenging things as they are. Role theory did not explain how change could be initiated by people already socialized into their given roles, where the motivation for change comes from, or why some behaviours changed more readily than others. Indeed, the focus of role theory was how people learned to conform. Failure to conform was usually defined as deviance.

The call for new role models was to some extent consistent with role theory, because it assumed that people would imitate the practices of others and would change their views when they actually saw women doing the nontraditional work. On the other hand, it moved away from role theory, because it called for women to be deviant. It was difficult to explain where this desire to change and these new models would come from, given that people were socialized into established roles. Certainly role theory considered the conflicts between roles, especially those between women's paid and unpaid labour. As Nancy Mandell (1986:213) explained, for employed women "Conformity to one role (staying home) may require deviating from another (going to work)." Furthermore, role strain may result when "our actual behaviour does not match our definition of the normative expectations contained in our role prescriptions" (213). But role theory offered little explanation for why women left their established housewife role in order to enter the labour force, for why roles changed.

Feminists faced similar problems when they tried to use role theory as a basis for their attack on what were defined as false stereotypes. They demonstrated that men's attitudes and behaviour — their roles — differed from those of women. This was consistent with the role theory that had extolled the virtues of women's and men's different but complementary roles. At the same time, however, feminists argued that people who fit into these roles were acting on the basis of false stereotypes. They argued that women's current roles did not reflect their real capabilities and that women were subordinated in these basically unequal roles. To solve this contradiction, feminists had to move beyond role theory; to argue that it was not false to assume that women and men often behave in different ways but that it was incorrect to assume that they must do so or that such roles are complementary.

Role theory failed to explain why some roles changed but others remained the same. A study done for the Economic Council of Canada, for example, accounted for women breaking out of their housewife role and entering the labour force primarily in terms of women "changing their perception of their role in society" (Boulet and Lavallée, 1984:6). At the same time, however, male and female attitudes about women's work, along with inappropriate choices women made about their education and perhaps the more appropriate choices they made about their children, were held to have kept women doing women's work at women's wages. There is no indication of how dramatic changes in one role are to be reconciled with the stubborn persistence of women's other roles.

Moreover, role theory gives no indication of how behaviour that contradicts the dominant ideology, or bears little relationship to that ideology, is to be understood. In their study of Alberta postal workers, Graham Lowe and Harvey Krahn (1985:16) found data to support the argument that "family situational factors are more important predictors of wives' employment status than are the gender attitudes of either spouse," suggesting that ideas do not always offer a primary explanation for women's work. An adequate theory would explain these different patterns of change.

Role theory, then, is not an adequate theory for explaining women's work. It does not offer a systematic explanation of how and why work roles develop or how and why they change. The emphasis on expectations diverts attention from the power structure. The emphasis on imitation and models diverts attention from structural factors and from people's efforts to bring about change. Although most feminist faculty members no longer use the term "Sex Roles" to label the courses they teach because they recognize the limitations of this approach, it is still common, especially in the popular press, to explain women's and men's work in terms of roles.

But the problems with the role concept are not limited to its analytical power. Even at the descriptive level, the concept is ambiguous. It is seldom clear what behaviour is included in the roles society makes people play. Sometimes the term refers to ideal behaviour; sometimes to actual behaviour. Sometimes it refers to behaviour as perceived or performed by the occupant of the role; sometimes to behaviour expected or desired by others. Such problems have led to endless elaborations — role sets, role conflicts, role strain, role sharing — which further reduce consistency in the use of concept. In addition, there is rarely a distinction made between the expectations of women and those of men. How women think women and men should or do behave may be fundamentally different from how men think women and men should or do behave.

Moreover, the behaviour that is described usually reflects that associated with white, prosperous, educated women and men. Differences related to race, class, age, and ethnicity are frequently ignored. Even if it could be demonstrated that unmarried Native Canadian women all hold similar views on motherhood and perform their motherhood work in similar ways, it is unlikely that their expectations and behaviour would conform to the patterns of white, Anglo-Saxon women married to the heads of corporations. Although such inadequacies in role descriptions could be overcome by developing a list of behaviour patterns for each and every class, racial, ethnic, and age group, the resulting multitude of behaviour groupings would undermine the whole concept of the consensus on appropriate behaviour that is central to the concept of role.

At both the descriptive and the analytical levels, then, role theory is inadequate. Theories and research based on the socialization of women and men into belief systems and appropriate roles have demonstrated that ideas are important and that women and men often think and behave in different ways. However, they have not provided a systematic explanation of how or why ideas and behaviour patterns develop or how and why they change. Recognizing the problems inherent in a theory that relies primarily on shared beliefs and roles to explain women's work, many feminists have begun to include ideologies, power inequalities, and economic structures in their analytical frameworks. Nevertheless, it is still common for many theorists to fall back on an explanation based on ideas when observed social patterns do not neatly fit into other theoretical frameworks.

Historical Materialism

When those feminist theorists who looked to Marx and historical materialism for theoretical guidance, considered ideas, they thought in terms of a dominant ideology that primarily reflects and serves the interests of a mainly male ruling class. These men's ownership and control of schools and the media, and their influence in courts and in politics, mean that their views and images predominate; that their way of interpreting the world is the one most widely disseminated and reproduced. Such views, images, and interpretations are not the only sources of ideas, however. As people work together to produce food, clothing, shelter, and babies, they are also producing their own ideas about how the world is organized, and why. Such ideas do not always coincide with the ideas of the men who control the political economy. Indeed, the contradiction between the world as many women and men experience it and the way it is portrayed in dominant symbol systems is often the source of rebellion and change.

As early as 1975, Dorothy Smith drew on Marx's and Engel's concept of ideology to explain both how the dominant system of ideas develops and how women are excluded from this development. For Smith, systems of ideas are not accidental or collective products representing universally shared values. "The work of creating the concepts and categories, and of developing the knowledge and skills which transform the actualities of the empirical into forms in which they may be governed" (Smith, 1975:354) is done in institutions such as schools, universities, broadcasting and publishing corporations, theatres and music halls, churches, and courts of law. These means of mental production have become the privilege of the "class which dominates a society by virtue of its control of the means of production" (355). The positions of members of this class give them the power to impose many of their ideas on others. "Because of their positions they view the world in particular ways" (356), ways that denigrate women and women's knowledge. Women have, for the most part, been "excluded from the work of producing the forms of thought and the images and the symbols in which thought is expressed and ordered" (354). Those women allowed to participate do so as individuals rather than as representatives of their sex. Men have authority as individuals because they are "representative of the power and authority of institutionalized structures which govern society" (362), not because they have innately special skills or knowledge.

The ideas of the ruling class tend to legitimate the current structures that benefit those in power; that serve to keep women doing women's work at women's wages. But, as we pointed out in *The Double Ghetto* (Armstrong and Armstrong, 1978:139), this does not mean that these ideas are necessarily consciously produced or that they never contradict the interests of those in power. "This class cannot simply invent ideologies: these ideas must correspond to some extent with the experiences of people in their daily productive activities" and in their relationships.

Those in power cannot simply impose their ideology, because there is another source of ideas for people in other classes and in the other sex — the ideas that "develop along with the practical activities of people in their daily lives" (138). Women and men are constantly creating their perceptions of and explanations for their worlds: "their ideas grow with their work, change with their work and, at the same time, affect their work."

It was this understanding of ideology that guided our research for

A Working Majority (Armstrong and Armstrong, 1983c). The women we interviewed repeatedly indicated that, contrary to what some functionalists suggested, they did not fully accept the dominant ideology, and that their experiences often proved these dominant ideas invalid. A bank clerk described how the ideology that said promotion was equally available to all was not borne out in her job — indeed promotion was restricted for women. She went on to explain that, although she often took over for her boss when he was away, she was still told that she did not have the skills to do the work (1983:17). These contradictions led her to question both the prevailing ideology and male authority.

We did not suggest, however, that each individual invents a whole new world view in a haphazard manner. As functionalist theorists have indicated, ideas developed along with the experiences of previous generations are transmitted through stories, images, and sanctions. But those ideas that do not coincide with women's and men's daily experience will be difficult to maintain. Moreover, these experiences are structured, in many ways, by the political economy. They are frequently structured differently for women than for men, because each sex is engaged, for the most part from the earliest years, in different activities. There are, nevertheless, many overlaps in women's and men's experiences and ideas. In their study of postal workers, Graham Lowe and Herbert Northcott (1986:95) concluded that "males and females who do the same work have very similar perceptions of their job, encounter similar degrees of work pressure, and report similar levels of job satisfaction." Moreover,

> males and females doing the same job reported almost identical psychological and physical distress, except the females experienced slightly more symptoms. In sum, we have demonstrated in general terms that employee reactions to their job are determined not by their sex but primarily by the nature of the job itself.

But women are more likely than men to be mail sorters and men are more likely than women to be letter carriers, and their different jobs help create different kinds of ideas.

This conception of the development and transmission of ideas included the assumption that ideas do not arise or spread in a smooth, linear fashion. Daily experiences are often contradictory, and so are the ideas that reflect and explain them. The classic example of the dialectical nature of experience comes from Marx's description of the free wage labourer. When working for wages, people are simultaneously free and unfree. They are free to sell their ability to work to any employer and they are free to direct the time spent outside paid employment. At the same time, however, they are forced to seek paid jobs from employers who largely control the market, and they are compelled to devote much of their time outside paid jobs to providing for their immediate needs. "So too are women freely compelled to marry and to have children and thus to do certain domestic work and, under certain conditions and within certain limits, labour force work as well" (Armstrong and Armstrong, 1983b:9).

Meg Luxton's (1980) interviews with Flin Flon women, carefully analyzed in *More Than A Labour of Love*, clearly illustrated these contradictions in women's work. Speaking of the labour involved in raising four children, a Flin Flon mother explained "I love them more than life itself and I wish they'd go away forever" (1980:87) . Other women described how their search for freedom from their parents' households led them to the dependency of a marriage contract. Similarly, a sewing machine operator interviewed for *A Working Majority* (Armstrong and Armstrong, 1983c) talked about the pride she took in her work, although she also described the job as degrading. Because many practical experiences in daily life are contradictory in themselves, it is not surprising that people hold contradictory views about what women can and should do.

Moreover, women's experiences often contradict the prescriptions of the dominant culture. A number of women we talked to in preparing *A Working Majority* said that "work outside the home didn't seem right to me" but were nevertheless forced by economic need to seek paid employment (1983c:39). These contradictions, as Peggy Morton (1972) pointed out in her groundbreaking article, can offer a basis for rebellion as women individually and collectively recognize that their position as interpreted for them makes little sense of their daily lives. In the process, new ideas are developed and disseminated, providing a basis for change.

Although the concept of contradiction is not found in functionalist theory, there is a contradiction inherent in functionalist theorists' efforts to demonstrate, on the one hand, that women often do behave in ways and do have ideas consistent with stereotypes while arguing, on the other hand, people who assume that women behave and see things in such ways are themselves accepting the stereotypes. We tried to address this problem in *The Double Ghetto* (1978). Using the concept of false consciousness, we argued that women's ideas may be false in the sense that they reflect a reality that is itself distorted, that segregates and distorts human nature. Women and men do different jobs. They develop different skills and different ideas. The pervasive division of labour helps create different perceptions of the world, as well as the conviction that the division of labour is natural and/or inevitable. These distortions are reinforced by the dominant ideology, which serves to justify the division of labour and simultaneously reproduces this division. The falsehood lies in assuming that these patterns are inevitable, not in believing them to exist.

A variety of studies indicated that women were often acting primarily on the basis of a rational evaluation of material constraints rather than, as some functionalists would argue, primarily on the basis of ideology. Patricia Marchak's (1973) research on women workers in British Columbia, for example, suggested that their low level of resistance must be understood largely in terms of their easy replaceability, rather than in terms of patriarchal ideology. The conditions of labour discouraged rebellion and encouraged particular views of women's work.

In contrast to many functionalist theorists, then, we were arguing that ideas are not simply imposed by men, by a particular class, or by families; nor are they exclusively the product of a one-way socialization or a mere reflection of economic structures. Rather, we maintained that people are active in the production of their ideas but that these ideas are circumscribed by the structures in which people function and by the work they do. Like the activities they explain, these ideas are often contradictory in themselves and may contradict aspects of the dominant ideology.

Because ideas reflect as well as affect work, it is not surprising that many women pushed into the labour force by economic need have changed their ideas about women's right to paid work. At the same time, because most women continue to perform the kinds of work, both within and outside of the labour force, that women have done for much of this century, it is not surprising that many of the old ideas about women's place have been retained.

In this framework, the explanation for changes in ideas does not rely primarily on individuals independently altering their perceptions of the world or on ideas independently altering work. Ideas and activities develop together. The process is dialectical and cannot be understood outside of the context of changes in the political economy. Variations in ideas among women of different classes, races, and ethnic groups can be explained, to a large extent, in terms of the different kinds of work and other life experiences they have. But they cannot be explained without also understanding how their changing consciousness and the exposure of contradictions influences and alters these experiences. Women and men act on the basis of this consciousness to create change.

This approach to understanding ideas and ideology is not without its own shortcomings that have still to be overcome. Perhaps most importantly, as cultural theorists in particular have pointed out, people do on occasion act primarily on the basis of ideas, and rational argument or evidence can have a profound impact on both consciousness and collective action. Although historical materialists would not deny that ideas can guide action or be changed through persuasion, they have not developed an adequate explanation of how, or under what conditions, this could happen. There is a general theory about how ideas change, but there has been no systematic explanation of the specific conditions that encourage the retention of old ideologies that do not coincide with current practices. Nor has there been an explanation of conditions that encourage the dominance of particular ideologies at different times, for different constellations of people. Joy Parr's (1987a:138) detailed study of a small Ontario hosiery town revealed how, even in a town where the ideology was contracted by women's position as primary wage earners,

> patriarchal ideology cast women as the primary custodians of kin, constrained the allocation of their labor between the household and market economies, and called forth a dependence of female kin upon one another for both domestic help and cash.

Any systematic theory should explain why ideology had a significant influence on, or at least provided justification for, the retention of women's household responsibilities, but had little effect on women's wage-earning position *per se*.

Moreover, little attention has been given to the problem of explaining why people act sometimes on the basis of shared racial characteristics, sometimes on the basis of shared class relations, and sometimes on the basis of shared biology. And although historical materialists have developed theories of ideas and ideology, especially in response to the critiques and evidence produced by others focusing on ideas, these theoretical tenets are invisible in much of their work. Ideas are too often ignored in the rush to expose material conditions and their influence.

Radical Feminism

For many radical feminists, it is women's reproductive labour that provides the key to understanding the dominant ideology and the differences between women's and men's perceptions. They, too, have drawn on marxist analytical tools — especially Marx's concept of alienation — to explain female and male consciousness.

Mary O'Brien argued in *The Politics of Reproduction* (1981:8) that it is "within the total process of human reproduction that the ideology of male supremacy finds its roots and its rationales." According to her, "human reproduction is inseparable from human consciousness" (21), and the origins of both patriarchal ideology and differences in male and female consciousness can be traced to "the historical discovery of physiological paternity" (21).

Once the male part in reproduction was established, men recognized their alienation from their seed. To overcome this alienation, men sought to appropriate their children. But in order to do so, they needed the cooperation of other men to ensure limited sexual access to women. This cooperation among men led to the development of social institutions and an ideology of male supremacy that served to reinforce abstract ideas about rights.

Unlike the alienation of the male seed in copulation, women's "alienation from their seed is *mediated in labour*" (32) and therefore, unlike men, women do not have to develop means of overcoming alienation; their labour "confirms their integration." Furthermore, "not only does this fact differentiate male and female reproductive consciousness, it differentiates male and female temporal consciousness" (32). At the same time, however, men's appropriation of children, which reflects their attempt to overcome alienation, creates contradictions for women's more integrated consciousness. This difference in the labour of reproduction, according to O'Brien, explains why women and men think and behave in different ways.

Although O'Brien's theory offered a way of understanding persistent differences in male and female ideas by linking these to the work of reproduction, it provided few clues to understanding change over time or differences among women from various races and classes. As we indicated in the Chapter Two, above, change for O'Brien is concentrated in two points — the discovery of male physiological paternity and the development of reproductive technologies — both of which seem to happen in a relatively independent manner, without conscious human struggle. Women in particular seem to have little to do with developing their own consciousness. The multitudes of developments in ideology throughout history and within societies are difficult to understand in these terms. Yet this consciousness was put forward as the basis of women's unified social consciousness. As Bonnie Fox (1988:166) pointed out in her critique of O'Brien, O'Brien "looked at relations; but the relations are between humans on the one hand and sperm and egg on the other." Although O'Brien talked about reproduction as a dialectical process, she gave little consideration to the contradictory nature of women's consciousness itself, and it was difficult to see how women could work to alter these differences in consciousness that lead to their subordination. Moreover, ideas were linked primarily to reproductive labour, leaving women's and men's productive work largely unexamined. As is the case in much of dual systems theory, "Marx's analysis of the dialectics of productive labour process is accepted as essentially correct" (O'Brien, 1981:15) and the relationship of productive labour to consciousness remained largely unexplored. We were left to assume that, because "productive labour is universal" (14), it encouraged similar world views in both sexes. Although O'Brien explained that men cooperated in controlling women's sexuality, and by extension their labour, she does not clarify the links between women's two kinds of labour and their ideas.

Psychoanalytic Theory

Some theorists have argued that it is necessary to understand not only those ideas that are consciously expressed but also the unconscious ideas that help shape our behaviour. Many of our ideas and practices are based on "things that each of us has either forgotten or never consciously known" (Horowitz and Kaufman, 1987:84). If it is the case that unconsciously held motivations and beliefs influence behaviour, then rational argument, role models, and even new hiring practices will have little impact on these perceptions of women's work. In order to change these ideas, some theory of the unconscious is required.

While relying on many of Marx's analytical concepts, some feminist theorists have also turned to Freud in order to develop an understanding of the unconscious and conscious ideas that keep women doing women's work at women's wages. Roberta Hamilton (1983:44) argued that "since our interest is not simply to understand the world but to change it, our theories are flawed if they do not include viable formulations about the nature of human beings." For her, the reclamation of work and of the productive process "must include *all* the activities in which we engage as we produce and reproduce our social world" (58). Theory must understand development as a physiological as well as a social process, as the ego developing in "response to the body's sexual maturation." Freudian theory can help explain how women and men were so tenaciously made into primarily heterosexual human beings and how femininity is socially devalued while masculinity is overvalued. Marx can help explain how these are not inevitable social processes but historically specific ones.

Hamilton suggested that Gad Horowitz's (1977) interpretation of Freud, which was built on the distinction between basic repression and surplus repression, provided "an analysis which explains the internalization of patriarchy." Some repression is required in all societies to "guarantee our humaneness" but in capitalist societies, surplus repression was necessary in order to ensure that most of our energies are directed towards toil. In Horowitz's explanation, patriarchy affects the structure of the nuclear family in capitalist societies. In such societies, the repression of non-reproductive sexuality is essential to production. More recently, Horowitz and Kaufman (1987:88) have argued that the "split between activity and passivity, so fundamental to our appreciation of masculinity and femininity, is a creation of a culture and society out of the undifferentiated unity of human *being*."

It is difficult to quarrel with Hamilton's argument that a theory of the unconscious is necessary if we are to understand women's work. In recent years, feminist theorists have been explaining more fully the connections between social structures and women's psychological makeup (see, for example, Boehnert, 1988; Caplan, 1985; and Caplan and Hall-McCorquodale, 1985) but the exploration of the unconscious from a feminist perspective has just begun.

Critical Theory

Both critical theory and discourse theory have drawn on marxist analysis to move in new directions in terms of subjectivity and ideology. Few English Canadian theorists, however, have explored the implications of these theoretical frameworks for women's labour. As Barbara Marshall (1988:209) has pointed out; "gender has not been the focus of critical theory." Nevertheless, Marshall (215) argued, because recent "critical theories have turned increasingly to a more synthetic examination of ideology, consciousness, language, etc. in response to the inadequacies of an analysis centered exclusively on the capital/wage labour relationship," they could overcome what she saw as the false dichotomies between structuralism and subjectivity as well as the reductionism of much socialist feminist theory (209). They could also, she maintained, get at the complex and contradictory nature of subjectivity and understand "how humans seek to come to terms with immediate circumstances and problems, the way in which structures limit their possibilities for action, and how in turn, they are reproduced by that action" (219) .

Marshall provided some examples of the complex, contradictory, and variable nature of human behaviour, as constrained by limited choices, and offered some interesting quotations from critical theorists. However, she provided few indications of a systematic explanation for the development of ideas and of how these ideas related to women's work. Nor did she indicate how women could struggle to improve their situation. Moreover, her characterization of socialist feminist theories as reductionist, dichotomous, and mechanical ignored much of the content of these theories, particularly in their more recent versions. Her critique also tended to ignore the differences in levels of theorizing that are central to understanding women's work in all its variable forms. She failed to make a distinction between theories that abstract overall trends and those that focus on processes within particular social structures. Nevertheless, few would quarrel with her call for a theory that "comes to terms with the complexity of our experience" (224); and few would argue that socialist feminism has done the job.

Conclusion

Out of these debates about and research on ideology and ideas has emerged a more sophisticated approach based on some fundamental points of agreement. Most feminists would agree that, while there is a dominant ideology that primarily reflects the interests of men in power, there are also wide variations in the ideas held by women of different class, racial, ethnic, and age groups. Most would agree that ideas cannot be understood apart from social structures and women's actions. Most would argue that we need, but do not have, an adequate theory of the unconscious and of socialization. And many would agree that ideas shape and are shaped by women's and men's daily experiences within and outside of the labour force. But there is still little agreement about how ideas and changes in ideas are to be systematically understood; about what these general agreements mean in practice. There are those who argue that ideas about women and men must be explained in a different way from ideas about class; others maintain that both kinds of ideas emerge simultaneously within the same system. There are those who argue that broad generalizations about the development and transmission of ideas are impossible to make; others claim that general rules can be exposed. There will always be historical, as well as class-, race-, and sex-specific reactions to these themes. And there are fundamental disagreements about whether the primary target should be ideas about women or should be structures of power, though few would argue that either strategy can be entirely ignored or that the two are easily separated.

What is needed is a theory that avoids the common practice of using ideas and ideology as the fall-back explanation, the one used when all else fails: "when in doubt, blame it on ideas." What is needed is a theory that explains the variations of ideas within a society as well as across cultures, a theory that explains not only the consistency in ideas about women's subordination, but also the maleability of these ideas when it comes to changing conditions, such as women's entrance into the labour force. What is needed is a theory that explains how some ideas change dramatically and rapidly, while others are tenaciously clung to, even when they are contradicted by reality. Such theory is necessary because, without changes in ideas, it is impossible to fundamentally alter women's conditions and relations of work.

Chapter Four

Beginning with Work: Economic Theories

Introduction

Although some feminist theorists focused on what women and men think, others began their analyses of women's work by concentrating on what women actually do. They looked at the jobs women have in the labour force, at the work they perform in the household, and at the relationship between these two kinds of work.

For some, this meant measuring and statistically relating a number of variables in order to determine the contribution of each to an explanation of women's work. Research based on this approach offered few explicit assumptions to guide the investigation. Rather, there was every indication that these researchers assumed that they were simply uncovering the facts and had no other purpose in mind. In this approach, the exposure of statistical relationships became the explanation for particular aspects of women's labour and little attempt was made to provide a systematic theory to help understand all of women's work.

Economists of many persuasions examined women's work. Although statistical relationships were a central component of their analyses, economists were more likely to have obvious explicit and implicit assumptions about the nature of capitalism and women's work than did those feminists who concentrated on revealing statistical connections. For the most part, economists were not primarily interested in changing women's condition. Indeed, in many cases their theories served to justify the *status quo*.

Traditional Economic Theories

In a study conducted for the Macdonald Royal Commission, Morley Gunderson (1985:220) suggested that economists' theoretical approaches to women's work fall into four basic categories: neoclassical taste perspectives, noncompetitive theories, statistical discrimination, and non-labour constraints. Theories that look to non-labour constraints focus on sex stereotyping and women's roles, approaches discussed in Chapter Three, above. Statistical discrimination theories also depend on ideas, assuming as they do that employers judge workers "on the basis of the characteristics of their group" (225). These theories share all the problems of idealist analysis in general, and have the additional problem of assuming that the perception of group characteristics is basically correct and that the only error is in the application of this perception to all individuals. Neoclassical and noncompetitive theories, however, are based on assumptions about economic factors, rather than assumptions about ideas, and therefore deserve further examination here.

As economists Marjorie Cohen (1982) and Martha MacDonald (1984) made clear in their surveys of the economic literature, the assumptions behind neoclassical theories make it difficult for these theories to provide an adequate explanation of women's work. For neoclassical theorists, market forces and rational choice prevail. Both women and men are viewed as having equal information and equal power in making choices that are designed to maximize utility and profit and that weigh leisure against further economic gain. The household is understood as a unit of consumption, rather than as a place of work, although analytical tools developed to explain the market are nevertheless applied to the household.

In an earlier study, Gunderson (1976:112) laid out the conclusions based on these assumptions:

> Job choices and opportunities for women are influenced by previous decisions, such as getting married and having children and level of education or training. Some women do choose occupations on the basis of complementarity with household activities. Part-time jobs, or those with flexible hours, enable many women to combine work in the market sector with work at home. Some women choose occupations that permit short or intermittent periods in the labour market, allowing more flexibility for

childbearing and child-raising, but often limiting advancement.

These economic theories exposed many of the links between women's paid and unpaid work. But they

> explain wage difference ultimately as a function of the division of labour, and the division of labour ultimately as a function of wage differences; that is they aptly describe the vicious circle women experience, but they do not explain its existence or function. (MacDonald, 1984:159).

Inequality is taken for granted, and it is not asked why it is women who must make the choice between parenting and a decent wage or a decent job. Constraints are accepted, not explained.

Power differences between women and men and between all potential workers and employers are ignored. So are differences in access to information about what choices are available. Rational choice is assumed to be reducible to economic gain, and leisure is assumed to mean the same thing for women and for men. Yet being home with the kids may well be leisure time for men and work time for women, and having children cannot be understood solely in terms of economic gain or loss. And, as Ann Duffy *et al.* (1989:28) recently concluded on the basis of their interviews with women, a number of social constraints (rather than rational choice) serve to encourage "women's tendency to allow extraneous events and significant others to make major life decisions for them."

In understanding the household as a unit of consumption, "the economist is able to say that activity within the household is rational because the household is maximizing its own utility" (Cohen, 1982:93). Those women who choose to work exclusively in the household do so because both women and men recognize that women are better utilized in the home. But the explanation given for this is that women's wages are lower. Not only is the argument circular, it is also contradicted by the facts when the explanation is presented in terms of choice. An extensive literature indicates that both women who stay home with their children and those who work for pay have very limited choices (see, for example, Armstrong and Armstrong, 1984a; Pryor, 1984). Many women who have paid jobs would rather stay home with their children and many of those at home would rather work for pay. Not only does this theory assume that women make a rational economic choice by staying home: it also assumes that this choice does not reflect decisions made by others over whom women have no control. This view of the household as a unit of consumption also means that "alternatives to production in the home (for example, day-care centres) will be considered only in terms of the cost and benefits of their impact on the market: not in consideration of total use of resources" (Cohen, 1982:93).

Neoclassical theory, then, has shown how inequalities are perpetuated, but not how they develop and change. When inequities in the market are addressed, they are seen as the product of ideas, usually called discrimination as taste. The causes of these ideas and the interests that they serve are left largely unexplained. Indeed, it is often assumed that competition will eventually make these ideas wither away because discrimination will become a taste that is too expensive to maintain.

Human capital theory comes out of the neoclassical paradigm. People are assumed to make rational choices about investing in their own development, their own capital. They make this investment by improving their education, their training, and their skills, and they reinvest when the demands for skills change. It is also assumed that people are paid on the basis of their marginal productivity, which is in turn related to their human capital. Women, then, are paid less because they have invested less in their own development for the market and because they are less productive. They are segregated into female job ghettos because they have only developed women's skills (see Armstrong, 1984). Segregation and low pay are women's fault because they have failed to learn appropriate skills or to obtain appropriate education.

The theory, however, is contradicted by evidence. As early as 1968, Sylvia Ostry (1968:45) found that "even after accounting for such differences in work year, occupational deployment and quality of labour between the sexes, there remained fairly sizeable pay gaps between male and female workers in Canada." On average, women have more formal education than men and are more likely to have taken courses that are directly job related (Gaskell, 1982). Furthermore, productivity is at least as much a consequence of the technology available and the organization of work as it is of the human capital employed. And, finally, there is little evidence to suggest that most women are employed in jobs that match their skills.

There is also a theoretical problem arising from the assumption made by human capital theorists that people are paid on the basis of their skills. As Jane Gaskell (1986) made clear, skills are socially defined and socially evaluated.

What is called skilled work varies with the sex of the workers, the power of the workers, the time, the place, and the economic conditions, indicating that skill is not merely some objectively determined set of characteristics, as human capital theory implies. In emphasizing this point, Gaskell seemed to suggest that there were no measureable components in skilled work and no objective criteria for separating skilled from unskilled work. At the same time, however, she described the various aspects of women's work, pointing out how skilled such work really is. Yet to argue that the work is skilled requires an agreement on at least some basic criteria for skill. This is not deny Gaskell's point that the same abilities and qualifications in women and in men may be differently valued and differently defined. Or to deny that some jobs that take years of preparation get dismissed as unskilled, primarily because many women have learned to do them and because women as a group have little power. Rather, it is to push the argument further by maintaining that skill can be better understood as part of work relations — relations in which women have little power — than a set of predetermined and easily agreed-upon or counted factors based on universal values.

The social definition of skills has become particularly obvious in the recent debates about how to achieve equal pay. For example, daycare workers need post-secondary education. They must change diapers and carry children. They require patience and understanding, as well as a familiarity with psychology and with the nature of biological growth. Yet they earn significantly less than garbage collectors, who require less formal education, whose work does not entail patience and understanding, and who do not face smells much worse than those created by dirty diapers. If skill determines wages, why is this the case? As these kinds of problems began to be exposed, fewer and fewer theorists turned to human capital theory for an explanation of women's work.

Segmented Labour Markets

The most popular approach in the category Gunderson calls noncompetitive theories was one that focused on segmented labour markets. This approach emphasized "the changing organization of labour demand," examining "processes which affect the differential labour force experience of various subgroups" (MacDonald, 1982:171).

Dual labour market theory understands the market as basically divided into two sectors. Jobs in the primary sector are characterized by relatively good wages and working conditions, opportunities for advancement, and job security. Those in the secondary sector, by contrast, are dead-end and low-paid. They offer little security and poor working conditions. White males constitute the majority of the employees in the primary sector; females of all races form the majority in the secondary sector, where many visible minority men are also found. Movement from the secondary to the primary sector is very difficult, since each sector draws from a different labour supply. Internal markets that allow promotion within the primary sector are shaped by technological developments, by the need for skilled workers, by ideas, by pressure from workers, and, most importantly, by the need for stability.

"Employers in both sectors rely on highly visible characteristics and assumed group traits when hiring employees" (Armstrong, 1984:29). Because there is a constant interaction between the characteristics of the job and those of the workers, employees eventually begin to display these traits even if they did not have them when they were hired for the job. A woman, for example, may be hired for a job because it is assumed that she has a secondary commitment to the labour market. The temporary nature of the job ensures that this is the case.

In this approach, "it was not poor choices but lack of choice that explained the division of labour by sex" (Armstrong, 1984:29). The problem was not women who failed to invest in their human capital but jobs that offered few opportunities, and employers who hired selectively for a segmented labour market. It was not assumed that rational choice and free market forces prevailed. Although the theory looked to factors other than individual choice for explanation, it left room for collective action.

Dual labour market theory was an improvement on human capital theory, but was more descriptive than analytical, especially in the versions that shared many neoclassical assumptions. It described different labour markets but did not satisfactorily explain how they come into being or how they change. Like neoclassical theory, it did not further our understanding of how women come to be slotted into particular kinds of jobs. Instead, it took the sex segregation of the market as given, or blamed the segregation on statistical discrimination, that is, on employers' ideas about the characteristics of workers. And it failed to explain why women and men in the same sector are paid different wages or why segregation by sex within industries and within occupations has "persisted even as more and more women demonstrate a primary commitment to the labour force" (Phillips and Phillips, 1983:87). Unlike some versions of neoclassical theory, it did not consider the relationship between the household and the formal economy.

Some of these problems were dealt with by more radical versions of segmentation theory. According to MacDonald (1982:177), segmentation theorists who used marxist analytical tools saw

> the origin of segmentation in a struggle between capital and labour to control the labour process: this is dialectically related to the momentum of capital accumulation which generates a monopoly sector of the economy and a general pattern of uneven development.

In other words, the segmentation of the market was explained in terms of the search for profits as well as in terms of workers' resistance to the deskilling of labour and to the increasing pressure to work harder for less money. Employers are seeking to reduce the expensive and powerful primary sector by creating more part-time jobs, by subcontracting work, by relocating jobs, by introducing new technology, and by reorganizing work. This results in more jobs in the secondary sector and more jobs for women.

Although this theory offered an explanation of why segmentation occurs, it did not provide an adequate explanation of why women end up in the secondary sector and why even occupations designated primary or secondary are further divided by sex. The concentration of women and visible minority men in the secondary sector was variously attributed to unions trying to protect themselves from these workers, legislation designed to protect workers, the inheritance of pre-existing group differences, ideas held by employers or workers, and "the role of capitalist expansion in creating (and eroding) semiproletarianized groups (groups not totally dependent on wage labour for survival)" (MacDonald, 1982:179).

This theory lumped women with other marginalized groups, a problem MacDonald called the "women and other minorities approach" (189). It thus failed to further our understanding of why women often do not fare as well as youth, immigrants, older workers, and visible minorities, or why the extent of marginalization has changed much more over time for these other groups than for women. It does not tell us why clerical workers are primarily women, rather than older male workers or immigrant men. It does not tell us why clerical work is a secondary rather than a primary job, nor why the Irish no longer do the least attractive jobs but women still do. Nor does it explain differences among women. Like other versions of segmentation theory, this version failed to link women's labour force jobs to their domestic work.

When it comes to women, all these economic approaches tend to fall back on explanations for women's work that have been fundamentally challenged by feminist research and theory. Economist Stephen Peitchinis (1989:21) has recently offered the following summary of economic answers to the old question of women's work:

Historically, much of the occupational segregation of men and women has been attributed to two realities: the *functional* reality in the work place, which involved long hours, heavy work, taxing work environment; and the *role differentiation* between men and women, which imposed on men the responsibility to labour in mines, on the land, in manufacturing processes, in transportation and construction in order to provide the means of subsistence for their families, while women specialized in work at home, including the bearing and rearing of children.

In other words, in the end the explanation is based on either biology or ideas. Although economic theories have exposed many of the links between women's domestic and wage labour, offered some explanations for why jobs in the market are segmented, and developed some approaches that recognize that people are active in making history, they have not provided a systematic explanation for women's work.

Statistical Connections

Many social scientists, including economists, did not begin with explicit assumptions or grand theories but instead concentrated on measuring and statistically relating various aspects of women's work. Explanations followed, rather than preceded, research, and the generalizations based on the data were applied only to the particular facet of women's work being studied.

This approach did provide some valuable evidence about relationships. For example, research by Allingham and Spencer (1968), Nakamura et al. (1979), Nakamura and Nakamura (1985), and Skoulas (1974) indicated that women's rising labour force participation could be related in some degree to general economic conditions and to such factors as earning potential, geographic location, age, immigration status, and social values. These factors were not the most critical, however. Female labour force participation was strongly related to the presence of young children in the home, to the level of women's formal education, and to husbands' income. More recent analysis indicates that the relationship between low female labour force participation and the presence of young children is weakening, as more women stay in the labour force after their children are born. Women are still more likely to have and keep paid jobs if they have high levels of formal education. In spite of the growing number of women who complete their post-secondary education, however, most women still leave after high school. Education, then, is not the primary factor linked to rising female participation in the paid work force. Rather, economic need, measured in terms of husbands' income, provides the best predictor of whether or not married women will have paid jobs (see Armstrong and Armstrong, 1984a:166-178).

In other words, this approach led to the conclusion that most women take paid work because they need the money, although it should be noted that these researchers seldom stated the conclusions in such bald terms. Instead, there was a tendency to indicate a pluralistic determination of patterns, a multiplicity of factors.

Work undertaken from this perspective also demonstrated differences among women. As early as 1975, Monica Boyd (1975:406) compared the situation of recent female immigrants to those of women born in Canada and of immigrant men. Her data led her to conclude that immigrant women

bear a double burden with respect to their status in Canadian
society: they are frequently classified as dependents upon entering Canada when *de facto* they make substantial labour force contributions; and, when they work, they are likely to find themselves in the
predominately female occupations, compared to male immigrants, and
in 'blue collar' occupations, compared to native-born women.

Boyd's (1980:21) more recent research indicated differences among immigrant women. Those who come here from the United States and Great Britain fare much better than those who come from Third World or Eastern European countries.

Although these statistical connections provided important groundwork for theory, they failed to provide complete, systematic explanations for women's work. Connections were often not explained at all. There was little attempt to explain why married women had an increasing need for income, why they had previously dropped out of the labour force, why it was women's work that varied so much during the last few decades and why it was immigrant women from particular countries who suffered more than either other women or immigrant men. As sociologist Cerise Morris (1987:124) has pointed out, "to state descriptively that people belonging to a given social category are statistically more likely than others to be located in a certain situation is not to explain *why* or *how* this is so."

The contribution of these approaches is also limited by the lack of explicit assumptions. It is clear that all research requires that some assumptions be made in selecting whom to study and what variables to measure. To examine, for example, the relationship between husbands' income and wives' labour force participation means that it has already been assumed that women depend, to a large extent, on the income of their spouses. But if these assumptions are not made explicit, it is difficult to evaluate them in relation to either theory or research.

Furthermore, such partial explanations encourage a very unsystematic approach, a buffet selection of various pieces of explanation that are either arbitrarily glued together or simply used in isolation to understand particular aspects of women's work. Often the various pieces contradict each other or only work in very limited situations. Explanations need to be connected in a systematic manner in order to foster the development of a complex and adequate understanding of women's work. This requires explicit assumptions and theory that works at more that the particular level.

Conclusion

As conclusions by Martha MacDonald (1984) and Marjorie Cohen (1982) have made clear, traditional economic theories have mainly served to justify the kinds of work women currently do, relying heavily on ideas, choices, markets, and skills to explain inequality. More recent economic theories have described a divided labour market, largely structured by the search for profit and workers' resistance to the pressures that result from strategies designed to increase profits. Although these theories are better than earlier approaches because they do not blame women or an "invisible hand" for women's subordination, they do not provide much explanation for why it is women who are so consistently segregated to the bottom of the job and wage heap. In part this results from the fact that economic theorists have not paid adequate attention to women's work outside the labour market.

Chapter Five

Production and Reproduction: Breaking Tradition

Introduction

For socialist feminists, a focus on women's work meant the application and transformation of marxist analytical tools. These theorists assumed that analysis must begin with the way people provide for their own food, clothing, and shelter, and for the next generation; with how they cooperate to provide for these needs; with the tools and resources available; and with the new needs that emerge as old needs are satisfied. Analysis begins here because these processes establish the outlines of any society. In a capitalist society, the drive to accumulate — or what we commonly call the search for profit — sets the broad conditions for all activities. This is not to suggest that the economy determines how history unfolds or what individuals do, but rather to indicate that these processes set the outer limits for human behaviour.

Indeed, what was particularly attractive about marxist approaches was the possibility for change. Those using marxist analytical tools were explicitly committed to fundamentally altering women's work. Marxism seemed to offer a basis for understanding labour that not only exposed the major forces shaping people's lives, but also saw people as actors in history. For marxists, the search for profit creates contradictory processes, and the conditions for individual as well as collective opposition. There is a logic to capitalist development, yet the contours of any particular society will vary with women's and men's efforts to shape their lives and the conditions they face.

For feminists, then, the appeal of this approach lay primarily in the emphasis on the social construction of inequality and on contradiction, in the systematic explanation for interconnected aspects of individuals' daily lives, and in people's active participation in structuring their work and ideas. But Marx and marxists had little to say about the particular nature of women's work and about the segregation of labour by sex. As theorists sought to apply marxist tools to feminist questions, these tools were criticized, developed, transformed, and, by some, abandoned.

Class and Domestic Labour

In contrast to those who began without explicit assumptions and with sophisticated statistical measures, many feminists in the 1960s began with a marxist framework, an assumption of inequality, and a commitment to change. For them, theory was central to action because it helped make visible the social structures and social relations that keep women in their place. It was the guide to what must be altered if women are to improve the nature and conditions of their work; a guide that had to be constantly reassessed as experience revealed problems with the theory and as women's work was transformed.

According to marxist theory, classes that develop along with work relations are the motors of change and are central to people's view of self and of consciousness. It is not surprising, then, that these feminists began their theoretical task by looking at women's work and class relations. Many focused on domestic labour because this work was done almost exclusively by women and was fundamentally different from the work done by either sex in the formal economy. It thus seemed to offer a promising clue to the specificity of women's subordination and to women's class relations.

But the task was far from simple. Marx's conceptualization of class was not always consistent or easy to grasp. Although Marx was clear that classes make history, he was less clear about how classes are to be understood. Unlike functionalist theorists, Marx did not fit people into classes by determining a set of easily measured characteristics such as education and income. Rather, Marx saw classes as being defined by a set of continually changing relations that, in capitalist societies, were primarily based on the ownership and control of the means of production. But, in a passage frequently quoted by feminists, Marx's close collaborator Engels mentioned the relations involved in creating the next generation of workers, without exploring the implications of these relations for class formation.

Interpreting and extending Marx in a variety of ways, feminists began to debate whether the relations that are part of producing and maintaining people in the household make all women a class that can work together for change. Does domestic work unite all women within a single class or are women divided by class relations that reflect those in the formal economy? If the formal economy is the key, how are women's class relations to be understood.

Although Charnie Guettel was not the first Canadian feminist to take this approach, it is appropriate to begin with her because she offered an orthodox interpretation and an uncritical application of marxist analytical tools. Her theoretical perspective was not particularly influential, but it is useful to examine it in some detail because it sets the stage for later developments and because, in spite of its limited impact, her kind of interpretation of Marx is often used when others seek to dismiss marxist analysis. In *Marxism and Feminism* (1974:52), she argued that woman's "double oppression exists in the fact that she is sustained by either her own or her husband's wages from outside the family to perform unpaid work in the home." The origins of and economic interests served by women's subordination and segregation are clear and identical. "Women are oppressed by men because of the forms their lives have had to take in class society, in which both men and women have been oppressed by the ruling class" (1974:2).

In the writings of Marx, productive labour done in the formal economy was the basis of class relations and revolt. Housework, Guettel (48) argued, is merely unproductive consumption and therefore can never be the basis for class opposition. In keeping with this perspective, she maintained that there are class differences among women that seem to reflect their husbands' relations to production. At the same time, she argued that "ruling class women were not the equal of ruling class men" because these women too did domestic work (14).

This double burden of domestic and wage labour she understood as capitalism's means of exploiting working people. The double burden serves to ensure a supply of both male and female labour while keeping wages low for both sexes. Therefore, in order to overcome their subordination as women, women have to work for the socialization of domestic work and enter the labour force. By entering the labour force, women can become part of the working class and there engage in class efforts with men to change the primary cause of their oppression, capitalism. Sex differences in the market position of women received scant attention from Guettel. Women are to become part of a sexless working class, a class that will struggle to transform the productive system and the state, which provide the basis for women's subordination.

Perhaps most significantly, Guettel demonstrated the limited usefulness to feminists of an interpretation of Marx that understood organized opposition strictly in terms of a single unified class struggle that is directly determined, like all other facets of daily life, by the search for profit in the formal economy. Her argument reduced women's subordination to a mere by-product of capitalism and offered no explanation for women's double burden other than capital's drive to accumulate. Women have two jobs because it is useful to capitalism. An economic base creates directly and automatically a superstructure that seems to include ideas about women's work, families, and domestic work. In her analysis, both women and men passively comply with the capitalists, who have everything their own way.

Yet, in marxist analysis, changes come from contradictions, from the dialectical development that is integral to the drive to accumulate, as well as from people's efforts to change their conditions. Although those who own the means of production are very powerful, capitalists do not have things their own way even if there is little organized resistance from the working class. The very search for profit creates contradictions and elicits the opposite of what was intended or sought. But the only contradictions in Guettel's analysis come at the end, when the inevitable development of capitalism create the conditions for women as productive workers and members of the working class to revolt. Women's liberation will follow automatically from the success of the working class struggle, given that women's subordination is caused by capitalism alone.

Contradictions were not central to Guettel's analysis, but her theory itself was contradictory. In her view, classes created by productive labour in the market are the only basis of change. Women are not a class because they are not united by their shared productive work. Rather, women are divided by the class differences derived from their husbands' paid work. Yet women, united only by their role in consumption, are to work together to socialize housework and overthrow the double burden that has been capitalism's means of exploiting working people. Guettel's conception of families was also contradictory. She argued both that families are created to serve capitalist interests and that "the working class needs families for survival" (20). Many would argue that families do indeed contain contradictions, but Guettel produced these two views of families without indicating how they could be reconciled within her analysis. The problem here, and throughout the book, is that she reduced everything to capitalism's unified needs and failed to consider not only contradictions but also the multiple facets of women's reproductive work.

For others beginning with marxist analytical tools and the question of women's class relations, the answers were not quite so straightforward. Although most assumed that the general conditions of women's work within and outside of the household are established by the search for profit, they did not view the drive to accumulate as automatically and directly creating ideas, families, resistance, or domestic work. Unprepared to accept a simple, deterministic, or uncritical interpretation of Marx, they argued that the basis for women's subordination is to be found in the household. What women do in the home was to be understood as work, not dismissed as consumption, and the roots of inequality were to be found in the conditions and relations of that work.

In her pioneering article "The Political Economy of Women's Liberation," Margaret Benston (1969) argued both that what women do in the home is work in the marxist sense and that this shared work makes women a class under the historically specific conditions of advanced capitalism. Citing the marxist distinction between use value and exchange value, she maintained that women as a group are responsible for the production of simple use values associated with homes and families that continue to function in a precapitalist form. Household labour as a separate form of work was created by the development of capitalism but continues in many ways as it did before capitalism was firmly in place. Unlike the paid work of men, which produces exchange value as well as use value, the unpaid work of women is valueless from the standpoint of capital because it produces only use value.

Benston added a historical dimension to the analysis of women's work, utilizing the distinction between use value and exchange value to explain how women's domestic work acquires its current content and meaning. Cut off from the means of directly producing what is necessary for survival, more and more people have become dependent on wages. More and more goods and services are purchased in the market — are commodified — although much of domestic labour remains outside this market exchange. The source of power and control is the market. Domestic labour, which does not directly produce for the market or command wages, thus acquires a secondary status and becomes a distinct form of labour under capitalism, which is based on exchange.

That women's domestic work does not directly contribute to profit does not, however, make it irrelevant to capital accumulation. Women's household labour fulfills "the need for closeness, community, and warm secure relationships" and stabilizes the entire economy by maintaining the ideal unit of consumption, which guarantees a demand for goods produced in the market (285).

Benston also argued that women's labour is useful to capitalism in another form. Some women participate in the labour market, although such participation is, according to Benston, transient and unrelated to the group definition. For Benston, this transient participation in the market results from women's primary responsibility for domestic work and serves to make women what Marx would call a reserve army of labour.

Benston was the first to use this concept in relation to women, arguing that women can be called on to fill vacancies in the job market and sent home to do their domestic work when their services are no longer required. The wages of men purchase the necessary labour of two people, and allow women to be hired to do low-paid work in the market when the demand for workers rises.

Because Benston saw women's two jobs as so integrally linked, she argued that fundamental change would have to occur in both the public and the private spheres for women's position to improve. Work done in the home would have to be done in the formal economy, and true equality in job opportunities outside the home would have to be established. Benston thought that neither of these goals were possible to attain within capitalism, because the formal economy could not absorb all these workers.

Benston thus offered a much more complex analysis than did Guettel of the relationship between domestic and wage labour, looking to both the reserve army and the distinction between use value and exchange value for an explanation of women's work. She did not, however, solve the problem of how to fit women into the class concept and thus theorize the change she saw as necessary. Although she argued that women already constitute a class on the basis of their production of use values in the home, her conclusions suggested that women are to become part of another class by eliminating their domestic work and joining the labour force on equal terms. What, then, was the use of declaring them a class by virtue of their household "labour"? If women's membership in a class of domestic labourers is the key to change, what are the conditions necessary for that revolt? If class is defined by relations and is not just a category, who are women revolting against: owners or men? Why has this class not already revolted? If capitalism defines women's work, what sense does it make to talk of domestic work as a precapitalist form? And how are class differences among women to be understood?

Like Guettel, Benston did not make the contradictions that are the basis of struggle in marxist analysis central to her explanation of change. She did not understand women's work as the result of past struggles between women and men or between workers of both sexes, and owners. As Meg Luxton demonstrated in the interviews she conducted in researching *More than a Labour of Love* (1980), and as we argued in "Beyond Sexless Class and Classless Sex" (Armstrong and Armstrong, 1983b), women's domestic work is essentially contradictory. Women are like the free wage labourer who is both free and unfree — free to change employers and free when not at waged work, but not free not to work for a wage and not free while at waged work. Women are freely compelled to marry and freely compelled to mother and, increasingly, freely compelled to take on labour force work. Because Benston did not make contradictions central to her analysis, it is difficult to determine from her work how or why this class of women who do domestic work will come together to change household work.

Benston was one of the very few in English Canada who argued that women constitute a class on the basis of their domestic work. Various other feminists have sought to understand women's class relations in marxist terms, but all have concluded that there are significant class differences among women.

In what remains a very powerful and complex piece, Peggy Morton introduced a new way of looking at women's domestic work, one that focused more on the production of people than on the production of goods. For Morton, women do not simply produce use values. They produce something that connects them much more directly to the creation of profit — labour power. The family, Morton maintained, is responsible for "the maintenance and reproduction of labour power" (1972:53). This "conception of the family allows us to look at women's public (work in the labour force) and private (work in the family) roles in an integrated way." Although domestic work means that "real contradictions exist for women as women. ... Women are nevertheless objectively, socially, culturally and economically defined and subjectively define themselves through the class position of their husbands or their family and/or the class position derived from work outside the home." Women do not, therefore, constitute a class but, rather, are divided by class differences. Lady Astor, Morton claimed, was not oppressed by her chauffeur, and it was doubtful whether Lady Astor's maid was more oppressed by her husband than by her employer.

Unlike Guettel and Benston, Morton made contradictions central to her analysis. Not only are there contradictions between the work women do within the home and the work they do outside it; there are also contradictions inherent in the nature of work in either place. The family serves capitalism by socializing children, repressing sexuality, and instilling appropriate hierarchical relationships through the education of future workers, but this is no smooth process. The very needs of the system create conflicting demands on the family as a unit, on women, and on children. These contradictions, Morton maintained, provide the basis for the development of strategy and struggle. Since male supremacy is structural, not just attitudinal, the struggle must be directed towards changing the system itself.

Although Morton offered an explanation for why people would revolt, she did not explain who would revolt. Would women unite, in spite of class differences, to alter the system, or would they work with men of their own classes to change social structures? Moreover, Morton offered a variety of ways to determine women's class differences, but did not make clear which factors were most important in shaping class relations for women.

Other feminists continued the struggle to understand women's class relations, each exposing more of the complexity inherent in women's position. Roberta Hamilton explored the different work experiences and life situations of women in peasant, craft, trades, and noble families during the transition from feudal to bourgeois and proletarian households. She argued that the development of capitalism increased class differences among women. "The women of the bourgeoisie were kept in physical comfort, in idleness and in a state of total dependence. Proletarian women lived out a continuous struggle combining working and mothering in their desperate and often futile struggle to ensure their families' survival" (Hamilton, 1978:93).

A marxist analysis that emphasized the importance of production explained these differences for Hamilton, but did not help us understand the persistent differences between women and men. To comprehend women's subordination, Hamilton argued, it is necessary to look at patriarchal ideology and at how biological inequality has been "translated into privileges not only for rich men but for all men" (104). The differences between women and men must be understood in terms of sex, not class. Changing the structures of capitalism would alter class relations but not necessarily sex relations. The transformation of relations between the sexes would require a separate, and different, struggle.

Others, too, maintained that there were class differences in the kinds of work women did in the home. Situating women within the family and the family within the dominant mode of production, Dorothy Smith argued that capitalism changed all women's work to personal service. But there remains a crucial difference between working class and middle class families. "The household for the working class woman is a means of meeting the needs of its members, and that is her work. Middle class women are oriented by contrast to the values and standards of an externalized order" (Smith, 1973:45). Bonnie Fox (1980) distinguished between working class and middle class women on the basis of household income and resources. Although both these views made it clear that not all household labour is the same, they did not tell us how to locate women in terms of class relations or what these class differences mean in terms of women's struggle for change.

In "Beyond Sexless Class and Classless Sex" (Armstrong and Armstrong, 1983b), we argued that what was needed was a concept of class that takes both domestic and wage work into account, and understands sex differences within classes as well as differences between classes. Unlike Hamilton, we assumed that all differences have to be understood within the context of the search for profit. Unlike Guettel, and like Hamilton, we assumed that there are differences between the sexes that are related to reproduction, and that will not simply disappear with the demise of capitalism. Like Smith and Fox, we assumed differences in domestic work but argued that these have to be connected to the paid work of women and men. Both the domestic and wage work of both women and men have to be considered in developing an understanding of class identities and class consciousness. We suggested that such an approach would expose the material basis for the subjective and objective antagonisms between the sexes within classes. It would thus help us understand the contradictions and classes that would either provide the potential for change or limit this potential. We did not, however, follow through on this suggestion.

Martha MacDonald and Patricia Connelly (1989) have developed a theory of class that takes all labour and sex differences into account. Applying this approach to their research on Maritime fishing villages, they demonstrated how an individual's class identity is influenced by her or his work history within and outside of the paid labour force, by family work patterns, and by sex. According to MacDonald and Connelly, both women and men are affected by spousal employment patterns and by relations between the sexes, albeit in different ways. People experience class not just as individuals in unequal productive relations that are divided by both sex and class, but also as members of household units characterized by unequal relations between the sexes. The search for profit not only shapes the environment, but also interacts with household relations and household strategies for survival. State policies influence, and are influenced by, actions in both spheres as well. These complex relations structure the content and nature of, as well as the possibility for, resistance. MacDonald and Connelly concluded that ''class shapes gender relations and gender shapes class relations.'' Their detailed analysis of a group of people who have collectively and individually struggled for change indicated both the complexity of class relations and the fruitful nature of this approach.

Joy Parr's (1987a) study of an Ontario hosiery town has also revealed complex class relations, relations influenced by the economy, by household structures, by sex divisions and patriarchal ideology. In a town where women constituted the primary labour force, ''some changes in thinking about women and men's roles and in the practice of domestic gender divisions took place'' (Parr, 1987a:138), but ''both managers recruiting a female labour force and women employees planning to accommodate wage work accepted as outside their agency the patriarchal ideology which made women more responsible for kin and which set definite limits on men's obligations within the household'' (139). Parr made it clear that any analysis of class must take this ideology into account.

As Bonnie Fox (1989:13) points out in her review of status attainment and social class theories,

> because women's situation is different from men's, some reconceptualization of class is necessary to accommodate gender differences. The realities of women's material conditions must be recognized as well as the possibility that a woman's class condition may not be exactly the same as her husband's.

Moreover, concepts of class have to take more than sex differences into account. As Patricia Connelly and Pat Armstrong have argued,

> class has to be reconceptualized through race and gender within regional, national, and international contexts. The static categorization of class that has been used in so much of class analysis does not capture the experience of gender, race/ethnicity or class. Class is dynamic and relational; it is the basis of change. Gender, race/ethnicity and regionality/nationality interact with class in various ways with one being more salient than another at different points in time. The problem for socialist feminism is to develop a theoretical account of these different types of oppression and

the relations between them with a view to ending them all (Connelly and Armstrong, 1989:5).

As feminists have used marxist concepts to understand the position of women, they have transformed these concepts. Each new exploration has contributed to the argument that work done in the home, including the work of bearing and rearing children, must be included in any notion of class. Each new exploration has increased our awareness of the complexity of class relations for both women and men. Although few would now argue that women constitute a class or that sex and class are separate issues, the most recent theoretical work clearly demonstrates that any conceptualization of class is inadequate if it does not take sex, domestic work, race, and region into account.

Value and Domestic Labour

Because Marx thought of class primarily in terms of productive relations in the market, those who were exploring women's class relations raised questions bout how women's domestic work was related to the search for profit and about whether or not women's work was productive. Although the debates surrounding these issues often looked like mere academic games, they were important because the answers helped indicate how women's domestic work developed and how easily women's work could be changed to reflect women's interests. Marx's analysis had indicated that productive labour was crucial to the creation of surplus value and how it was governed by what he called the law of value. Basically, Marx showed how the difference between the labour actually done by a worker and what the worker is paid is the main factor in the production of profit, or surplus value. Owners are constantly searching for ways to increase control over workers and to decrease their wages, because this is the main means of making profits grow. And owners have to struggle to increase profits, or they will be overcome by the competition. If domestic work were productive and contributed to accumulation, then it too would be governed by these laws and would be crucial to profit growth.

Benston (1969) argued that domestic work is valueless from the standpoint of capital because it produces only that which is used in the household, not that which is exchanged in the market. It therefore does not directly contribute to making a profit and is not subject to the law of value, or to strategies designed to increase profit. Morton (1972), on the other hand, argued that women's work contributes directly to making a profit when they bear and rear children or care for and feed men. Women's work is productive because it contributes to the production of labour power, the essential ingredient in the production of surplus value.

But, according to Marxist analysis, productive labour is that which is directly exchanged for a wage in order to produce surplus value. Given that housework is not directly exchanged for a wage, it is not productive in this sense. Marx used the distinction between useful labour and productive labour to distinguish between the usefulness of the work in general and the social relations involved in the labour. All labour is useful but only productive labour produces surplus value. While capitalists may be interested in what happens to other forms of labour, they *must* be interested in what happens to productive labour, because without productive labour there is no capitalism. Capitalism, for Marx was the social formation in which labour power is normally bought and sold as a commodity. Without the distinction between productive and useful labour, the forces that govern the capitalist mode of production cannot be understood. To define domestic labour as productive does not help us understand more clearly how housework develops, because the laws Marx outlined do not directly apply (see Armstrong and Armstrong, 1983b).

Wally Seccombe (1974), in an article that launched what came to be known as the domestic labour debate, maintained that domestic labour is not productive in the marxist sense of the word. Nevertheless, he argued, domestic work is necessary under capitalism because the commodities bought in the market for domestic consumption, and thus for the reproduction of labour power, have to be converted into their final form before they can be consumed. For Seccombe, what distinguishes domestic labour under capitalism from domestic labour in other kinds of economies is that it contributes to the creation of the commodity called labour power without having a direct relation to capital.

To develop his argument, Seccombe returned to Marx's analysis of the mystification inherent in the wage. According to Marx, wages appear to be equivalent to all the work done on the job but in fact are equivalent to the cost necessary to maintain the workers — the cost of getting them back to work the next day — not to the entire value of their labour. Indeed, surplus value is based on the difference between the labour performed by workers and what they are paid for the work. According to Seccombe, wages appear to be exchanged only for labour performed on the job site, but in fact are also exchanged for the labour needed to reproduce labour power. Because domestic work is part of the latter, it creates value that is equivalent to the production costs of its maintenance, despite the fact that it does so under the privatized conditions of the household. But although Seccombe's (1974:9) argument that domestic labour "contributes directly to the creation of the commodity labour power while having no direct relation with capital" helped clear up the confusion created by those who wanted to see domestic work as productive, it did not clarify the relation of domestic work to the laws Marx outlined for labour performed in the market.

What became clear in the debate was that domestic labour is not equivalent to wage labour. Although women contribute to the production of the commodity of labour power, they are not paid a wage and they do not have a labour contract. Unlike the exchange between employers and paid workers, that between husbands and wives is variable and arbitrary, subject to interpersonal bargaining. Unlike the free wage labourer, wives do not sell their ability to work for a wage, even though their domestic work may seem to be a condition of their access to men's wages. The exchange based on a marriage contract and a non-wage relationship has very different implications than that based on a labour contract and the payment of a wage.

As mentioned earlier, wage labour is free labour in the sense that wage labourers sell their labour power to employers of their choice for a definite period of time in return for a wage. Time not at work is their own and they are free to exchange employers when they wish and when conditions permit. Because employers pay workers a wage, they constantly seek to reduce necessary labour time in order to increase surplus value. Domestic labour, on the other hand, is not free labour. Because women's household work is based on social and emotional as well as economic commitments, it is difficult to change employers freely. The relationship between wives and husbands is different from that between employers and employees, both because it is seldom a strictly economic relationship and because it involves all, rather than part of, women's daily life. There is little distinction in terms of either time or space between women's work and non-work time. Because women working at home are not paid a wage and thus do not produce surplus value, there is little interest on the part of capitalists in reducing the necessary labour time by increasing women's domestic productivity. More efficient housework may make it easier for women to do their jobs and may make life more pleasant for all household members, but it does not directly result in either increased wages or, more importantly for employers, increased profits. Marx revealed the mechanisms that affect wage labour, but the same rules do not apply to domestic work, because this is a fundamentally different form of labour.

The early domestic labour debate virtually ignored women's wage labour, concentrating instead on women's contribution to the reproduction of male workers. In response to critics who pointed out that his analysis failed to explain the relation between women's two kinds of work and that Marx's laws did not seem to apply to domestic work, Seccombe (1975) argued that there is an average domestic labour time, just as Marx said there was an average wage labour time. Seccombe (89) defined the average domestic labour time as "that labour time necessary to convert the average wage into the average proletarian household, at the average price of wage goods." Using this definition, he maintained that when real male wages fall, women can compensate for the decrease either by intensifying their household work or by entering the labour force to "supplement the family income." There is an "exchangeability of labour time embodied in wage goods for domestic labour time." Women made a "value trade-off" when they take paid work, compensating for the increased cost of the replacement for their domestic labour with their additional income. But this explanation did not seem to go much further than that offered by traditional economic theories that understood women's labour force participation in terms of rational choice.

Seccombe's argument that domestic labour creates value and that there is necessary domestic labour time did not explain women's movement between the two kinds of work. If both forms of labour are equivalent, why should women take on a second job? In fact, it is precisely because domestic labour and wage labour are not equivalent that they are not interchangeable. Domestic labour is both more flexible and different in form from wage labour. Pregnancy, for example, does not have an equivalent in the market. Clearly, some household labour can be replaced by purchased goods and services, but most women do not replace all their domestic work with Big Macs and cleaning services. They simply leave some work undone, do some work less often, and lower the quality of their other labour. These strategies are not readily available to the wage labourer and they do not suggest that there is an average labour time for domestic work. Indeed, it is because women who do domestic work are not creating value, are not directly subject to the law of value, and do not have an average domestic labour time that they can take on paid jobs, forming a reserve army of labour. In many cases, it is because floors can go unscrubbed and beds unmade, because women can vacuum less often and make hamburgers for supper that they can enter the labour force. And it is because women cannot easily get someone else to have their babies and because women take on the major burden of domestic work that they do not provide the same kind of labour supply as do men (Armstrong and Armstrong, 1983b).

But to argue, as we did in "Beyond Sexless Class and Classless Sex" (Armstrong and Armstrong, 1983b), that domestic labour does not create value and is not subject to the law of value is not to argue that the law of value does not influence this work. Under capitalism, all work is transformed by the law of value, even work that is not paid for. As Seccombe (1980) pointed out in a later article, the household is influenced by both the retail market and the labour market. Household production varies in response to wages and to the demand for labour, as well as to the prices and availability of goods and services. Households respond by varying the number and spacing of children, as the declining birth rates in Canada attest; by varying the wage labour of women, of men, and of children, as the recent reduction in youth and rise in female labour force participation indicates; by adjusting purchases, as the growth in fast-food services demonstrate; and by going into debt, especially, these days, in order to buy housing. But the impact is not the same direct one that is seen in the case of wage labour. It is also not simply one-way. Decisions made by household members about jobs and children influence the market.

Although the domestic labour debate failed to demonstrate that work in the household creates value and is thus subject to the laws Marx outlined, it nonetheless furthered our understanding of women's work. In summarizing the contributions of the debate, Seccombe (1987:190) concluded that

> we went some way towards comprehending the special character of housework as a labour process, the reasons for its obscurity under capitalism (via its role in the daily and generational reproduction of labour power) and, most importantly, the forces shifting the proportions of paid and unpaid labour which household members, as a group, perform in making ends meet.

In struggling through the implications of applying the law of value to domestic work, the participants in the debate revealed the opposite of what was intended. They showed how domestic labour differs from wage labour but is related to it. This provided the basis for an argument that it is the special nature of domestic work that creates the flexibility for, and thus the possibility of, women constituting a reserve army. But, as Seccombe (1987) pointed out in his recent reassessment, such an argument fails to explain why it is women who do the domestic work, and it relies much too heavily on economic determinism for an explanation of all women's work.

Domestic Labour and Wage Labour

The domestic labour debate was a rare occurrence in English Canadian feminist development, in that it focused almost exclusively on theoretical issues and took place largely in an international context. While this theoretical debate was raging, many other English Canadian feminists were attempting to relate theoretical and empirical work, concentrating on explaining the connections between domestic and wage labour, and testing the usefulness of Marx's analytical tools. They explored the possibilities of Marx's reserve army concept; they looked at the impact of economic change on women's two related jobs, at the labour process in both kinds of work, and at women's participation in unions. These interests overlapped and became increasingly integrated as each group learned from the other, and as women's work in both the private and the public sphere changed.

Benston (1969) had introduced the notion that Marx's theory of the reserve army would help explain women's labour force work. Ceta Ramkhalawansingh (1974) demonstrated how the First World War served to accelerate the movement of single women who had not previously worked outside the household into the labour force and encouraged a temporary influx of other women as well. But it was not until Patricia Connelly's book *Last Hired, First Fired* (1978) was published that the application of this concept to women was fully explored.

Using the reserve army concept in the way it was interpreted by Harry Braverman (1974), Connelly explained how reserve armies develop and distinguished between the various forms the reserves take. For Marx, it is the search for profit that largely determines the supply and demand for labour. In order to increase profits, capitalists seek to sell more and to pay less for labour. They introduce new technologies and new means of organizing work as a way of reducing their reliance on workers. In the process, they throw workers out of work and create what Marx called a floating reserve of workers that is available for employment in other areas. The new commodities introduced by capitalists in order to increase sales often serve to eliminate old forms of labour and old means of survival. Those who work in these threatened areas, such as agriculture, form a latent reserve that has not previously been employed in the labour force but can become available in the future. Those who work in marginal areas of the economy where employment is extremely insecure form a stagnant reserve of irregularly employed workers.

These reserves are essential to capitalists in two ways. First, the pres-

sure from a large number of people without paid work helps employers control currently employed workers and helps keep wages down.
Workers are more hesitant about rebelling because there are other workers to take their place, and the competition for jobs keep wages low.
Second, the reserves ensure that workers are available when new industries develop, or demand grows in other areas.

Connelly (1978:21) explained the conditions necessary for the creation of a reserve army of labour. Workers must be cheap and they
must be available for employment. Moreover, they must compete with
each other for jobs. Women are available as an ''institutionalized in-
active reserve army of labour'' because the development of capitalism
initially ''defined women out of the capitalist labour market,'' leaving
them responsible for the production of what Benston called simple
use-values in the home (Connelly, 1978:26). Women are a cheap source
of labour, because the value of their labour power ''is not determined
by the means necessary for the maintenance *and* reproduction of their
labour power; at most it is the means of subsistence necessary to maintain their labour power'' (32). In other words, women's wages are
lower than those of men because men's wages are based on the assumption that they have a family to support. Women's wages, on the
other hand, are based on the assumption that women are partially
supported by men or at least have only themselves to support. Finally, the sex segregation of the labour market not only ensures that wom-
en compete with each other for a limited number of low-wage jobs;
but also puts pressure on men's wages because men fear replacement
by women, who will work for less.

Research by Connelly and others indicated that women fulfilled these
three conditions for a reserve army. The lower labour force participation rates of women clearly indicated that women formed a latent
reserve, in the sense that they were not currently employed in wage
labour. The Second World War provided the clearest example of how
this reserve could be drawn into the labour market when it was required, as female labour force participation rose from 24.4 percent in
1939 to 33.2 percent in 1945 (Armstrong and Armstrong, 1984a:21).
The rapid drop in the postwar participation of women indicated a great
deal of flexibility in that particular reserve. The steady increase in female participation rates since the war supports the claim that many
women did indeed constitute a latent reserve. Those who had not previously worked for pay became available for employment in the market.

There can be little doubt that women were a cheap source of labour
and that most women competed with each other for jobs in a limited
field (see, for example, Armstrong and Armstrong, 1978, 1984a; Fox

and Fox, 1986; Goyder, 1981; Ornstein, 1983; and Statistics Canada, 1985). Based on his investigation of wage differentials between the sexes, Michael Ornstein (1983:46) concluded that "by far the largest factor in explaining women's low wages is their concentration in low wage occupations." Moreover, there is evidence to suggest that "men's wages decrease significantly with increases in the percent of the workers who are female" (Fox, 1981:52). In other words, women's low wages put a downward pressure on men's wages. And finally, studies of both bank work (Lowe, 1987) and teaching (Prentice, 1977) indicated how women can be used to replace men (whose labour is more costly and who may be reluctant to work in such jobs), especially when new technologies and new labour processes are introduced.

But this strong supporting evidence for certain aspects of the reserve army concept did not prevent criticism. Three major, and related, problems were raised. The first challenged the theory on the grounds that women have moved permanently into the labour force and thus do not constitute a reserve because they do not provide a flexible supply of labour. That women's unemployment rates have not been higher than those of men during recessions was also seen as evidence against the reserve army concept, given that it was assumed that women would be sent home when large numbers of men were unemployed. The second kind of critique maintained that the theory fails to explain differences among women; that it is more descriptive than analytical and does not offer a universal explanation for women's work. The third problem has to do with the failure of this concept to explain why it is women who form a reserve and who do the household labour, and with the portrayal of women as mere passive pawns.

Those who used the relatively permanent movement of women into the labour force, and women's unemployment rates, as evidence against the reserve army theory could do so only by adopting a very simplistic and deterministic interpretation of the theory. It is true that some understood the reserve army theory to mean that all women responded like yo-yos to the demands of capital for labour, jerked into and out of the labour force at the whim of employers. But, as Connelly explained, there were different kinds of reserves. As a latent reserve similar to that provided by agricultural workers, women could be expected to move into the labour force and stay there as their alternative forms of support disappeared.

In the nineteenth century, married men and single women were the first in Canada to be forced into wage labour, the first to lose access to the means of directly producing for their own needs. Some married women also worked for wages from the earliest period of capitalism because they had no alternative way to acquire food, clothing, and shelter, or support for their children (Armstrong and Armstrong, 1983b; Connelly, 1982). However, as Bradbury's (1984) research on nineteenth-century Montreal households and Cohen's (1988) research on dairying in Ontario demonstrated, many married women had access to the means of producing for their survival or of gaining income without entering the labour market. Not only did married women do considerable necessary labour in the home that prevented them from searching for wage labour; they also grew food, sewed clothes, did laundry, took in boarders, or did other domestic labour that made it unnecessary for them to sell their ability to work for a wage. Some also produced goods for sale in the market. Such alternatives do not mean either that most men earned a family wage that supported their wives and children, or that most married women were completely or even primarily dependent on a male wage. They do mean that women were supporting their own reproduction in a way that allowed them to combine this work with the labour they had little chance of escaping — the bearing of children.

More recently, married women have been losing access to the means of production and to alternatives to wage labour. State regulation combined with the high cost of land and the low cost of substitutes make it impossible for most women to raise chickens in the backyard or save money by making their own preserves. With the mechanization of housework, household labour time has been reduced somewhat, and women have lost their boarders because it is easier for individuals to survive on their own. At the same time, male wages have not kept up with prices and more and more women have entered the labour force in order to maintain their families' standard of living (Armstrong and Armstrong, 1984a; Pryor, 1984). Many members of the latent reserve of married women, like the male agricultural workers of a century ago, have been forced to sell their ability to work for a wage since their alternative means of survival have disappeared. Many have moved relatively permanently into the labour force and can no longer be described as constituting a latent reserve that can easily be sent home when no longer required.

But the dramatic increase in female labour force participation rates does not mean that the reserve army theory is no longer relevant in explaining women's work. Connelly described three kinds of reserve armies. The latent reserve of women previously without paid work has largely been drawn into the market, but many women still form a floating reserve of workers who move from job to job or into and out of the labour force mainly in response to changes in capital's demand for labour. In addition, some women belong to a stagnant reserve of irregularly employed workers, especially in what has come to be called the underground economy.

Building on the work of Connelly, we argued that it is primarily as part-time workers that many women constitute a flexible pool of labour, a floating reserve (Armstrong, 1984; Armstrong and Armstrong, 1988). In the mid-1970s, feminists began documenting an increase both in the number of part-time jobs and in the proportion of women doing part-time work (Armstrong, 1984; Weeks, 1977, 1980; White, 1983). By the time of the most recent Census (Statistics Canada, 1988:Table 4), slightly more than 30 percent of women in the labour force did not hold jobs that are mainly full-time, full-year.

This increase in part-time work, we maintained, largely reflected new technologies and new work organization introduced by employers to reduce labour time (Armstrong and Armstrong, 1988:81). It also reflected the shift of employment to the tertiary sector. A variety of research studies had revealed how employers benefited from the division of work among part-time workers. Much of the work in the service and trade industries is easily divided into separate tasks and separate time slots. Periods of high demand vary over the day, week, and year. By hiring employees who only work during peak periods, employers can significantly reduce labour costs. Many jobs require little formal on-the-job training and rely on skills most women have already learned at home (Bellew, 1982-83). Women workers, therefore, are easily hired, easily fired, and easily replaced. Employed for short periods of time, they can work at speeds and under conditions that would otherwise be intolerable. High output with few errors is also possible if women are employed for relatively short stretches of time (Bayefsky, 1985; Weeks, 1977). Part-time workers are not only more productive; they are also cheaper. One reason is that they are paid only while they are actually working. Also, state regulations and collective agreements rarely require that part-timers receive fringe benefits, pay equity legislation has little effect, and part-timers are rarely unionized and are seldom paid for overtime (Canadian Advisory Council on the Status of Women, 1982). Moreover, computers, which are within the price-range of most employers, can dramatically reduce the cost of hiring part-time employees, since they can be used to organize and simplify pay, scheduling, hiring, and work organization.

However, as Julie White (1983) and, more recently, Duffy *et al.* (1989) made clear, women do not simply respond to capital's demand for labour. They make choices and develop strategies that manipulate the part-time work that is available in order to juggle their two kinds of work. Most women who do part-time paid work indicate that they do not want more hours of paid employment. Although this argument is a very important addition to deterministic interpretations of the reserve army theory, it should not be forgotten that these choices are very much limited by women's domestic responsibilities and by the work that is available. Many of the women who currently say they do not want full-time jobs might change their minds if good, affordable childcare were available, if they had less housework to do, or if the jobs they now do part-time were more attractive. On the other hand, if more household income were not required, many women would choose not to take any paid work while their children were young. Whether by choice or by necessity, women who work part-time for pay form a flexible, floating reserve.

Another, stagnant reserve is formed by women who are irregularly employed, many of whom are immigrant women employed in the underground economy. In *The Seam Allowance*, Laura Johnson and Robert Johnson (1982) showed how immigrant women's responsibilities for childcare, combined with the skills they had and the language skills they lacked, served to create a vulnerable reserve of women available to do largely unprotected work in the home. More recently, Carla Lipsig-Mummé (1987:44) explored the "exceptional increase in precarious and fragmented employment, and in homework, at the expense of full-time employment, in all manner of industries and service." Roxanna Ng (1986:269) has documented how job counselling and placement services shape immigrant women into "special commodities: a special kind of labour" that is cheaper, provides fewer choices for workers, and forces immigrant women to compete for a limited number of marginal jobs.

By adopting this more complex and sophisticated interpretation of the reserve army theory, feminists have shown how this theory can be used not only to explain how some women continue to constitute a reserve army of labour, but also how differences among women can be understood and how the concept of resistance can be incorporated into the theory. This version also offers a different way of examining the unemployment data that are used as evidence against the reserve army approach. Women's official unemployment rates did not exceed those of men during the most recent recession in part because many women became underemployed, with fewer hours of work, rather than completely unemployed; in part because women were employed in female-dominated sectors where they did not compete with men and where the recession was slow to be felt; and in part because many women who are unemployed simply disappear from the unemployment data (Armstrong, 1984).

As useful as this theory is in its current, qualified form, it does not offer an explanation for all of women's work. But then, it was intended to provide a way of connecting women's domestic and wage labour — of understanding what was called women's secondary labour in the market — and not as an all-encompassing theory of women's work. The reserve army concept was only one of Marx's analytical tools. Like functionalist theory, the reserve army approach took women's responsibility for domestic work for granted, and did not try to explain why it is women who do this work. Unlike functionalist theory, however, it challenged rather than accepted this responsibility. Moreover, contrary to what critics claimed, it offered an explanation for the development of different kinds of flexible labour pools and drew out the relationship between the demand for labour and the supply of women workers.

The Labour Process

The early studies exploring the theoretical concepts central to the domestic labour debate and the reserve army discussion relied primarily on statistical data to determine the location of women in the market and the division of labour in the home. But feminists grew increasingly dissatisfied with the limitations of data that provided only a broad overview both of what jobs women did and of the connections between women's two kinds of work. They also became increasingly disillusioned by a domestic labour debate that seemed to have reached a dead end. In an effort to investigate more concretely the implications of the theory and to move beyond the mere categories of occupations or tasks given in the statistical analysis, feminists began to use qualitative research techniques to examine the nature, conditions, and relations of women's work within and outside of the household. Such research, which involves a great deal of time and considerable financial resources, became more feasible as feminists began to win their fight to legitimate research on women's work.

As feminists began to explore what women actually did every day, they drew heavily on the theoretical approach outlined in Harry Braverman's *Labor and Monopoly Capital* (1974). Braverman expanded on Marx's analysis of the nature, conditions, and relations of work — of what was termed the labour process — through an examination of transformations in modern capitalism. Simply put, Braverman started from several basic assumptions taken from Marx, according to whom capitalists are constantly trying to increase profits by offering more and more goods and services for sale in the market and by reducing their costs of production, which has an impact on the way work is structured.

As a consequence of the efforts to sell more, goods and services previously produced directly in the household become available for sale in the market sector, often at a lower price. At the same time, alternative means of producing these goods and services disappear. This process, described as commodification, makes everyone more dependent on wages. In order to increase profits, capitalists seek to decrease their reliance on labour power by both reducing work time and increasing control over workers. Jobs are broken down or fragmented into quickly learned tasks. This fragmentation means both that the whole job can be done more quickly and that workers are easily replaced. Work is reorganized so that each task requires little skill and little knowledge of the entire production process. This separation of conception from execution, combined with the deskilling of jobs, makes workers easier to replace and increases owners' control over the work and the workers. to increase control over workers. Technology and organizational strategies not only increase productivity, but also ensure that each employee is working to the full extent of her or his physical capacity, a process Braverman called intensification of labour.

Although Braverman's pioneering work was central in shifting the focus of theoretical and empirical examinations of work, his analysis was widely criticized. Many pointed out that, in his effort to draw an "objective" picture, he neglected to devote sufficient attention to the notion of contradiction that is so fundamental to marxist theory. Consequently, he neglected to devote sufficient attention to worker resistance. Braverman underestimated the prospect of new skills emerging as old ones were eliminated, and failed to consider the possibility that some of the technology designed to increase control could end up providing a basis for workers' resistance. Although Braverman looked at women's clerical jobs, he did not connect such work to women's other jobs in the household, nor did he make sex divisions in the labour force integral to his analysis. He seems to have romanticized the nature of the craft work done in the past, and to treat skill as simply an objective, agreed-upon category, rather than a socially constructed one determined to a large extent by power relations.

In spite of these valid criticisms, Braverman's analysis offered important tools for the exploration of work. Feminists used the work of both Braverman and his critics as a basis for examining women's jobs and, in the process, helped transform the theoretical understanding of the labour process.

Using research done by others as evidence, we argued in *The Double Ghetto* (Armstrong and Armstrong, 1978) that the kinds of developments outlined by Braverman were transforming household labour. Commodification had reduced some labour in the home while making women more dependent on male wages and, increasingly, on their own wages. These changes not only altered the power relations between women and men; they also made women's work more isolated and thus less visible and less obviously necessary. Many of the old skills, such as those involved in canning, baking, and sewing, were no longer required, and women had fewer products to show as the result of their labour. The new skills that women developed, such as the management of children's schedules and of money, were very difficult to see and appreciate. The new technology and new commodities that made it possible for one woman to do the household labour by herself often made wage work necessary for married women. The loss of assistance from children who were at school and domestic servants who found other work had intensified women's domestic work. The addition of another job in the labour force had the same consequence. Women were working harder and longer because they had two places of work.

Although we examined the contradictions created by women's two kinds of work, we, like Braverman, failed to explore the contradictions inherent within the domestic labour process. Also like Braverman, we did not investigate the resistance of women to domestic labour relations and we tended to treat skill as entirely objectively determined rather than as largely a product of struggle.

It was Meg Luxton's *More Than a Labour of Love* (1980) that offered the first full description of women's domestic labour, and took both Braverman and his critics into account. Distinguishing between ''the way particular women organize their daily work and the patterns that are essential to the occupation housewife'' (1980:12), Luxton demonstrated how domestic labour ''is profoundly determined by capitalist production and functions at the heart of the social relations integral to the capitalist mode of production'' (17). But, as she explained, contradictions were inherent in production for exchange, in the connections between the two kinds of labour, and within domestic labour itself. Women are not mere pawns in the process of capitalist development. They use their resources, like pregnancy, as a basis of power, and they also develop out of these contradictions strategies for shaping their lives. ''Women's labour in the home is one of the ways in which the working class adapts and modifies the effects that external market forces have on its household'' (17).

In a later article based on the same research, Luxton (1981:21) argued that her comparison of what she called middle and working class women suggested that, although all married women constitute a reserve army, "the content of their experience may well be very different depending on their class background and their current class positions." A follow-up study (Luxton, 1983) of the women she initially interviewed indicated that conflicts over domestic responsibilities were developing between wives and husbands as economic pressures pushed more and more women into the labour force. Again she found a variety of patterns in women's responses to these conflicts, patterns that she related to differing ideologies as well as to changing material conditions. In sum, Luxton's research on domestic work revealed how the drive to accumulate shapes household activities and relationships, but it also indicated how women and men take specific actions that influence their daily lives.

While Luxton was interviewing women in Flin Flon about their unpaid domestic labour, others were using qualitative techniques to examine women's paid work. Laura Johnson and Robert Johnson investigated the factors contributing to the maintenance of paid work performed at home, as well as interviewing women about the nature, conditions, and relations of their work. They reported how the women, mainly immigrants, who sew garments in their own homes

> are forced to accept such conditions as fluctuations between 12-hour workdays and slack times with no work and no pay; piecework rates that are not disclosed until after the work is done; basic rates of pay set far below those paid to workers inside the factories; and penalties for work considered by employers to be substandard. (Johnson and Johnson, 1982:60)

Although conditions in the garment factories are not good, they are better than those experienced by the homeworkers, women who work for pay while at home. But immigrant women with young children or responsibilities for other family members have few choices about taking the work. They often cannot speak either of Canada's official languages; they have few recognized skills that are highly valued; and they often entered this country as dependents (Estable, 1986; Seward and McDade, 1988). Johnson and Johnson, in *The Seam Allowance* (1982), did not explicitly use Braverman's analysis, but their descriptions of homework clearly revealed techniques designed both to control workers and to reduce the amount paid for labour. They outlined how the search for profit creates this form of labour and how immigrant mothers' vulnerable position forces them into a reserve army available to do this work at these wages, under these conditions.

Like *The Seam Allowance, A Working Majority* (Armstrong and Armstrong, 1983c) did not explicitly acknowledge that it was guided by Braverman's approach, but his theoretical framework is clear in our analysis of interviews with women who do the kinds of paid work that most women do. The evidence from these interviews exposed many of the trends of deskilling, fragmentation, and intensification that Braverman described. At the same time, however, they revealed such contradictory tendencies as the emergence of some new skills and the development of resistance. Moreover, the interviews not only recorded clear patterns in women's paid work, but also indicated variety from job to job and from woman to woman. We

> were impressed by the sense of humour, cheerfulness and coping strategies of women who work in dull, repetitive, low-paid, uncomfortable, even dangerous, dead-end jobs; impressed by the commitment and pride that they bring to jobs classified as unskilled or low-skilled; impressed because they are cheerful, committed and proud in spite of a shrewd awareness of the value placed on their work and of their future possibilities; impressed by their desire to be fair, especially to their employers and supervisors, to see the other point of view even though they not infrequently face arbitrary, unnecessary rules and sexual harassment; impressed, indeed, overwhelmed, by the organizational skills they display in juggling the responsibilities of two jobs; impressed by the resistance that sometimes bubbles up in spite of their sympathy for their employer, the burden of two jobs and a realistic assessment of the large reserve of unemployed women waiting and willing to take their paid jobs; impressed by their growing union membership and their consciousness of many major issues, especially the consequences of new technology. (Armstrong and Armstrong, 1983c:215-216)

In short, our interviews painted a complex, detailed picture, besides elucidating some general trends.

By contrast, Charlene Gannagé's (1986) study of women garment workers explicitly set out to test the usefulness of Braverman's approach. Her study of a small garment factory revealed many of the processes that Braverman described. However, she criticized Braverman for "treating the labour process and the family as independent spheres," for viewing "the family solely as a unit of consumption and not an integral part of the capitalist labour process that reproduces labour power in the home," and for "viewing women solely in economic terms as a reserve army of labour" and thus failing to explain "why women, as women, are employed in certain low-paying sectors of the economy" (1986:12). In an essential transformation of Braverman's thesis, Gannagé's research demonstrated how gender is used by owners as a form of control. As well, she showed how important families are in shaping women's alternatives and how families create different alternatives for women of different ethnicities. Her study challenged the notion that families serve only to either support or confine women. Instead, she exposed the contradictions inherent in families, which simultaneously offer crucial support and help keep women in their place.

Joy Parr's study of the recruitment of immigrant women for an Ontario factory further enhanced our understanding of the skills involved in women's work and the way these skills are integrated into the labour process. A knit-goods firm recruited women from abroad and prepaid their passage to Canada. The "firm wanted that combination of judgment and dexterity which allowed workers simultaneously to maximize volume of product and quality to make the most efficient use of the equipment and generate the fewest possible seconds. The smallest flaw, of no significance in woven fabric, easily spread the length of a knitted garment" (Parr, 1987b:533). Yet the owner described the skills involved as "limited." The women came to Canada largely because their prospects in Britain had been reduced both by a general slump and by unions fighting to protect male jobs. However, although greater prosperity, fewer unions, and a shortage of skilled workers meant improved possibilities for women here, immigrant women were locked into their jobs by the scarcity of job opportunities outside the community. They were "unlikely to get good hosiery work and to evade their debt elsewhere" because knit-goods manufacturers combined to prevent such moves. "More importantly, they would be leaving behind a range of other advantages which, as skilled female wage-earners, they were less likely to secure elsewhere" (Parr, 1987b:538). Parr's work, then, suggested that market skills could help increase women's power and alternatives, but also that employers' strategies were designed to limit this power as much as possible.

In the early 1980s, the Social Sciences and Humanities Research Council of Canada funded three research projects designed to combine quantitative and qualitative techniques in order to conduct case studies that would further explore the complex relations between domestic and wage labour, focusing on the labour processes in each sphere. Patricia Connelly and Martha MacDonald initiated a series of studies that looked at male and female labour both in households and in the formal economy. In the first study, they compared the strategies developed by both women and men in different fishing communities to survive the pressures exerted on them by the development of capitalist relations. Their evidence suggested

> that women's wage labour has been crucial in maintaining this form of production and that this has been profitable for the corporate sector of the industry, keeping wages and the price of the raw material low. It has also preserved rural communities as general holding tanks for reserve labour, and kept wages low in the whole regional economy. (Connelly and MacDonald, 1983:67)

They showed how women's labour within and outside of the household is crucial to family survival and how men and women coordinate their labour in order to ensure the survival of the family as an economic and social unit. Equally important to the overall trends encouraged by capitalist development are regional differences in the impact of capitalism, and differences between the coping or resistance strategies developed by women and by men. Connelly and MacDonald's research exposed differences not only from region to region, but also from woman to woman, indicating how groups of women are often used as reserve armies competing against each other.

The case study of the families of Hamilton steelworkers undertaken by June Corman, David Livingstone, Meg Luxton and Wally Seccombe showed how labour relations in a large, urban community are like, and unlike, what Connelly and MacDonald described in their studies of Maritime fishing villages. The Hamilton interviews with both wives and husbands promise a rich source of material about both women and men in terms of their relationship to domestic labour. In a recent publication based on this research, Livingstone and Luxton (1989) showed how ideas about the male breadwinner role were both perpetuated by current divisions of labour and challenged by changes in women's labour force participation in general and by the movement of women into steel in particular. This research both revealed variations in strategies and demonstrated how developments in the steel industry shaped individual lives on and off the job.

Our case study of a major metropolitan hospital indicated tendencies similar to those described in the other two research projects. Although the hospital is funded by the state, organizational techniques designed for capitalist enterprises have been introduced into the hospital to save money (Armstrong, 1988). Much work has been reorganized to break down jobs into smaller, easily learned, and easily controlled tasks. More part-time labour is utilized and nurses "float" from unit to unit, an internal reserve army. Jobs are segregated by race and ethnicity as well as by sex, with immigrant women and women of colour relegated to the bottom of the hierarchy. The intensification of labour has spilled over into relations in the home, as women increasingly fight with their husbands and children and struggle to juggle two jobs. Pressures at home also influence women's paid work.

Here, too, there are contradictory tendencies, with some jobs expanding in terms of skills, or some aspects of jobs becoming more skilled, as old skills are eliminated. This study, like that of Connelly and MacDonald, allowed us to compare women, in this case women who do different jobs within the hospital. We saw that, as is the case in Maritime fishing villages, women face common pressures but, at the same time, there are increasing differences among women, even among those in the same job category. The experience of older and younger female workers are increasingly different, offering different opportunities and choices. The segregation of jobs according to race and ethnicity helps create and reinforce attitudes about superiority and inferiority. Like Connelly and Macdonald in their Maritime study, we were pushed to explore the consequences of state policies and programs. Unlike them, we were in a position to explore the different conditions faced by state employees (Armstrong and Armstrong, 1988). We were trying to draw out the connections, for both women and men, between labour in the market and labour in the household.

Such case studies have allowed a continual interplay between research and theory, with each informing the other. In essence, they have confirmed the general tendencies outlined by those involved in the domestic labour and reserve army debates. At the same time, they have indicated a great deal of variation from region to region, from class to class, from race to race, from woman to woman. And they have encouraged the development of theory that takes both contradiction and resistance into account. As the research has progressed, theory has become more complex and sophisticated, less deterministic and simplistic. Yet the research has raised at least as many questions as it has answered. It emphasizes the need for, and our failure in, theorizing differences within classes among women from different racial and ethnic groups, and among women of different ages. Little attention has been focused on ideas, ideology, and culture. Although contradiction is a central feature of the analysis, there has not been much progress in figuring out which women, under what conditions, will revolt, and who will be their allies in this struggle. And, finally, the attempt to link the labour process in the market to the labour process in the home has just begun.

Technology

As feminists began focusing on the labour process, new microelectronic technologies were starting to reshape women's jobs. It is not surprising, then, that feminists began to explore the impact of technology on where women work and on the nature of the jobs they hold.

Heather Menzies's pioneering case studies indicated that microelectronics would have enormous impact on women's paid work, eliminating jobs in areas dominated by women, cutting off career advancement, increasing managerial control and supervision by machine, encouraging the growth of paid work performed in the home, and endangering women's health (Menzies, 1981, 1982, 1983). Although her research supported Braverman's thesis, there was little discussion of theory in her work.

Margaret Benston (1983) did offer an analysis of the development of microelectronics, as well as some empirical research on the impact of this new technology. She argued that new jobs would appear, but that many would be routine, monotonous jobs precisely because this was what the technology was intended for. These were the jobs that would go mainly to women. The relatively few highly skilled jobs that will emerged would go primarily to men. Like Gannagé's study of garment workers, Benston's analysis of microelectronics demonstrated how important sex divisions are to the structure of work and of technology.

Labour Canada's study *In the Chips: Opportunities, People, Partnerships* accorded with the findings of Menzies. Although the study contained little theoretical discussion, it described the very different views held by labour and management concerning the consequences of microtechnology for employment. Employers' groups argued that "while there are undoubtedly some ill side-effects of the revolution, it must be realized that some short-term ill effects are more than offset by long-term benefits." Union representatives, on the other hand, maintained that "if we do not provide our members with an awareness and tools needed to deal with this challenge effectively, we will surely be beaten by this looming threat to our employment, income and way of life" (Labour Canada, 1982:36).

Labour Pains used this research and an analysis of data on the labour force to argue that these opposing views were not surprising. "The drive to accumulate pushes employers to raise productivity and to lower costs, particularly labour costs, to increase control over the labour process and thus over workers. Microelectronic technology enhances their ability to do all these things'' (Armstrong, 1984:139). As the unions maintained, the technology is designed to reduce both the number of jobs and workers' control over the labour process. But, as the employers argued, there are new possibilities created by the new technologies.

There are choices to be made, but the technology is not neutral. Technologies are making it increasingly possible to fragment work, not only in terms of tasks but also in terms of location. At the same time, technologies that permit production in response to order or demand, and which allow products to be quickly varied, encourage an entirely new structuring of the labour process. Old hierarchical lines of authority may be flattened out, with middle management jobs eliminated and work teams developed. Although they could improve workers' power and conditions, these trends are less likely to be felt by women, given that so many women are now involved in jobs that require neither recognized skills nor a need to understand the entire labour process.

Although studies of the labour process encouraged theories about the impact of technology on paid jobs, there was little theoretical discussion of the technology used in the home (Armstrong and Armstrong, 1985). Meg Luxton (1980) compared the technology available in the homes of three generations of Flin Flon women and looked at the impact in household work. Much more theoretical discussion is necessary, however, in order to develop a better understanding of the conditions under which such technology is introduced, and its effects on household relations.

Conclusion

This chapter about theories that rely heavily on marxist analytical tools is so lengthy because most feminist theoretical development in Canada, as well as much of the empirical research on women's work, began with this approach. The debates about the nature and relations of work within and outside of the home, and those about the relationship between work in both spheres, have moved far beyond a simple application of marxist analysis. They have been heavily influenced by the critiques of both non-marxists and marxists, as well as by changes in women's work. They have revealed the interpenetration of the so-called private and public spheres of the household and the formal economy, the importance of sex divisions to developing an understanding of class divisions, the impossibility of explaining production without reference to reproduction, and the necessity of connecting the labour processes in domestic and wage work. Guided by a broadly defined marxist framework, detailed research studies have challenged some marxist assumptions while confirming many of the general trends indicated by the marxist approach. Each new exploration of women's work has exposed the complexity of class relations among people divided not ony by gender, but often by race, ethnicity, region, and time as well. Many of these debates have ceased to command a great deal of attention, but they have provided the basis for a more sophisticated understanding of women's work, raising important questions for further debate. Perhaps the most significant lesson to be learned from the theoretical developments outlined here is that debate is essential to furthering our understanding of women's work.

Chapter Six

Women as Victims, Women as Actors

Introduction

Those who began their analyses with marxist analytical tools were often accused of failing to recognize women's collective and individual efforts to shape their own lives. But those who used a historical materialist framework were not alone in a tendency to assume that women were passive. Many feminists concentrated on documenting women's passivity and on explaining why and under what conditions women submit. As women's labour force participation continued to grow and as feminists continued to develop a more sophisticated analysis, however, more and more theory recovered and analyzed women's struggles for change. Feminists have become increasingly concerned with understanding why, and under what conditions, women will resist, and who they will join with in their struggles.

Understanding Passivity

Whatever they identified as the primary cause of women's powerlessness and passivity, most theorists traced the low level of collective and individual resistance to the family. Margrit Eichler (1973:49), for example, argued that, because non-employed housewives are personal dependents, they will display the characteristics of personal dependents, ''will be very submissive, will attempt to please and to control the master indirectly by manipulating him emotionally, whenever possible.'' When, as Eichler later argued, ''the industrialization of house-work and the generally perceived greater attractiveness of working at a paid job rather than being a housewife due to increased financial independence, social contracts, greater public esteem, and increased self-esteem'' lead women into the labour force, ''the old pattern abrupt-ly shifts'' (Eichler, 1983:195). With greater access to a variety of resources, women's power within the household will increase. Con-sequently, they will no longer display the characteristics of personal dependents; they will no longer be submissive.

Although Margaret Benston (1969) would probably have agreed that women's characteristics are related to their domestic work and would certainly have agreed that labour force participation is an important strategy for increasing women's power, she based her explanation of women's submission not only on women's work in the household but also on their work in the labour force. For Benston, women's pas-sivity will be changed only by creating equality in paid employment and by socializing domestic work — unlikely developments under capitalism.

Other theorists looked to women's bodies for an explanation of powerlessness and passivity. For example, the Women's Liberation Movement (1972:114), in its 1970 brief to a federal government com-mittee on abortion law reform, began by arguing that ''a major factor that kept women in this secondary role was the fact that women had no control over their own bodies. They are tied to the vagaries of na-ture.'' The involuntary nature of childbearing and its consequences made women dependent on men within families. Coupled with men's desire to control female sexuality, women's reproductive capacities limited their possibilities for resistance and encouraged submission. Reproductive technology and women's right to control their own bod-ies were seen as providing the key to, as well as the basis for, resistance. As Mary O'Brien (1982:255) explained, ''Female reproductive cons-ciousness is radically transformed by the development of reproduc-tive technology.'' In the same work, however, O'Brien went on to point out that this transformation ''has not yet been subjected to sus-tained theoretical critiques from a materialist perspective.''

Linked to the argument that the imperatives of nature provided a basis for male control over female sexuality was the analysis that at-tributed female submission in general to male attitudes and fears about women. Gallup polls have indicated that a majority feels that women should stay home to care for their children (Boyd, 1984:12) and that female labour force participation harms family life. Throughout the 1950s and 1960s, such polls indicated that only a minority thought women should be given an equal opportunity to compete with men for paid jobs. Such attitudes, combined with male fears of competition, were thought to provide an explanation for women's limited participation in unions (see, for example, Rands, 1972) and for their passive acceptance of women's work at home and in the labour force.

It was not only male ideas about women that were blamed for female passivity. Women were also blamed for holding such ideas about themselves. Indeed, Gallup polls suggested little difference between male and female attitudes in some areas. A woman, as Sarah Spinks (1972:80) explained, "internalizes a definition of maturity which is the early acceptance of quietness, obedience, and poise." Such ideas are socialized into girls within the family and, when girls become mothers, "there is a rather subtle mechanism by which mothers absorb the personality of their children." As indicated in Chapter Three, above, various strategies were suggested for developing alternative male attitudes and female self-concepts — consciousness-raising groups, different role models, changed media images, research, and the abolition of the family.

Early in the debate, Peggy Morton (1972:53) argued that analyses seeking to explain why people act to bring about change

> must be based on an understanding of the contradictions within the family, contradictions which are created by the needs that the family has to fulfill, of the contradictions within the workforce (contradictions between the social nature of production and the capitalist organization of work), and the contradictions created by the dual roles of women — work in the home and work in capitalist production.

For her, women's submissiveness arose from their work in both spheres, and their resistance would grow out of the contradictions within and between these two kinds of work.

Impressed by Morton's approach, we argued in the original version of *The Double Ghetto* (Armstrong and Armstrong, 1978:181) that "the rapid growth in the labour force participation of women has created contradictions in women's work experience, contradictions that contribute to their changing attitudes toward themselves and their work." We proceeded to outline what we thought these contradictions were, and suggested that they provide the basis for women's current resistance, individually in the home and collectively in the labour force. But, like Morton before us, we did not examine concrete struggles in order to determine the usefulness of our theory.

All these approaches pointed to conditions that contribute to women's submission to, and perhaps complicity in, their subordination. But they did not explain why, how, and under what conditions particular groups of women have resisted. Many of these theories tended to be functionalist, in that they explained women's passivity in terms of its usefulness to the system or to men, or as a direct consequence of their bodies, of work, or of culture. When women's struggles were recorded, limitations or negative consequences were often emphasized. Few of these theories examined how women may fight for conditions that are in their short-term interests, only to discover that such conditions are harmful in the long run. And few considered how these conditions may simultaneously maintain and undermine the interests of men and/or of capitalism. Moreover, these theories tended to lump all women together, without theorizing how women in different classes and in different racial or ethnic groups may develop different forms of consciousness and different strategies for action. In addition, they tended to leave aside questions of whether strategies will lead to individual or collective gains or forms of resistance. And, finally, there were few theories that explored how work in the home is connected to work in the labour force.

Explaining Revolt

As more and more women moved into the labour force, as women's membership in unions grew, and as the women's movement developed in numbers and strength, the focus of theory and research shifted from explaining and documenting women's submission to recovering and analyzing women's active resistance. As O'Brien (1982:254) put it, "Feminism is the history of resistance to male exploitation" and, increasingly, feminists have made such resistance integral to their analysis.

This is not to suggest that no theorist had examined women's collective efforts to make change. Historians in particular have recorded women's involvement in unions. *Women at Work, Ontario, 1850-1930* (Acton *et al.*, 1974), an early publication of The Women's Press, included two articles that examined women's participation in unions. The article by Alice Klein and Wayne Roberts (1974:214) emphasized "the dichotomy between the official view and that of working women themselves," stressing that many women were actively involved in unions and in strikes. In their conclusion, Klein and Roberts (252) raised some important questions for theory:

What was the degree of feminine consciousness and that of class consciousness and how were they related? What was the effect of such factors as the degree of intermingling of the sexes, and the classification of occupation in the interaction of class and feminine consciousness? What were the mainsprings of feminist consciousness in the productive and social process? How have they changed over time as women's occupations become more and more distinct from those of male workers?

Such questions remain central to theory today.

But another question that arose as a result of Klein and Roberts' research has been partially answered by historical developments. They asked "what explains the relative incapacity of women workers to generate a sustained leadership that could have enabled them to utilize and penetrate the mainstream of radical and social movements of the time?" (252-253). Today, the emergence of the women's movement along with women's rising and continuous labour force participation have contributed to the development of just such a sustained leadership. As Maroney (1987:86) demonstrated, "the radicalization of employed women has profoundly altered the organization and ideological balance of forces" within the labour movement.

Another article in *Women at Work, Ontario, 1850-1930* described women's involvement in the Toronto Dressmakers' strike of 1931. Using this example of women's resistance, Catherine Macleod (1974) explained male workers' hostility towards women primarily in terms of the threat posed by lower female wages. Women's weak position in the union was attributed to their reserve army status. However, she also saw ideology as playing a central role. "Women were thought of and thought of themselves as transient workers." This perception did not contradict reality, given that "the majority of women did not work, and those who did usually did so only until they were married" (324).

Although a number of articles recorded specific examples of women's efforts to create change, it was not until the late 1970s that resistance became a central part of theory and a large number of feminists began to analyze women's collective efforts to change their conditions of work. The articles brought together by Linda Briskin and Linda Yanz in *Union Sisters* (1983), Julie White's *Women and Unions (1980)*, the Bank Worker Collective's *An Account to Settle* (1979) and Elaine Bernard's *The Long Distance Feeling* (1982) all indicated common, contradictory patterns. Both male attitudes and fear of competition have often encouraged men to exclude women from, or control women in, unions. At the same time, women's domestic responsibilities and intermittent participation in the labour force have made continuous participation in unions difficult. Women nevertheless have been and continue to be active in and to benefit from unions. These publications also suggested that men have sometimes supported women in their struggles or have supported equal pay for women as a means of protecting their own jobs from cheaper female competition.

More recently, Ruth Frager's (1989) examination of Ontario garment workers in the 1930s indicated that men were willing to countenance separate organizations within the labour movement for Jews, but denounced separate organizations for women as divisive. Madeline Parent (1989) has recounted how, in Quebec during the same period, some male unionists were important allies for women textile workers. Such research reveals the contradictory and complex nature of men's strategies and women's responses in unions.

While men have occasionally supported women in their struggles, women within and outside of the labour force have frequently supported men in theirs. As Luxton (1982:117) pointed out, housewives in Cape Breton, Joliett, Sudbury, Hamilton, and Flin Flon actively participated in strikes for higher male wages. "They know that their husbands' struggles for higher pay, shorter hours and better benefits directly affect their work and their families' lives. They have also demanded that men, and the male dominated unions, take women's concerns into account during negotiations."

Such collective action often benefits women, at least in the short term. Moreover, it often politicizes them in a way that makes them less ready to accept subordinated status within or outside of the household, and more ready to take action in other areas. On the other hand, it may lock women into an even more dependent position within the household. In examining women's struggles for better employment conditions, the authors cited above have gone beyond documenting women's active resistance to expose the complicated nature of their demands and victories as well as their alliances with men.

Other publications have explored women's resistance to men and to the demands of their own bodies. Angus McLaren (1978), for instance, showed how women workers in nineteenth-century Canada shared their knowledge and took individual, independent action to resist male control over their bodies and to limit the size of their families. The articles brought together in Still Ain't Satisfied (Fitzgerald et al., 1982) document women's collective struggles for reproductive rights, for limitations on pornography, for the right to express their sexual preferences, for reductions to their domestic work and childcare responsibilities, and for the prevention of domestic violence and sexual harassment. O'Brien (1981) cites women's struggles for abortion and day-care, and against rape and battering.

An analysis of these struggles has been put forth by Nancy Adamson *et al.* in their study of the modern Canadian women's movement, *Feminist Organizing for Change* (1988). They argued that the women's movement has led to important legislative changes, to a new public consciousness, to an "increased acceptance of women's rights as well as increased awareness of women's inequality," and to the "self-organization of women themselves" (1988:4-5). Important as these changes are, the women's movement "has not transformed the society in fundamental structural ways, although it may have changed the rhetoric, the ideology, and perhaps even the expectations of society — changes not to be underestimated but also not to be confused with a more far-reaching vision of women's liberation" (6).

On the basis of their historical analysis, they proposed a model of feminist practice based on the concepts of mainstreaming and disengagement. Mainstreaming refers to attempts to work within existing structures to bring about concrete and immediate changes. Disengagement, by contrast, is focused on a longer-term vision involving major structural and social changes, taking feminists "outside the structures and views accepted by the majority of people" (177). For these authors, both strategies "are necessary components of any strategy for social change" but "an over emphasis on one or the other seriously undermines the possibility of making change" (176). In a more recent article, Briskin (1989) argued that it was necessary to maintain an effective tension between these two strategies. Her analysis suggested that socialist feminist practice in Canada has been somewhat more successful than that in either the United States or Britain because Canadian socialist feminists have been involved in both mainstreaming and disengagement, varying their strategy depending on time, place, and issue. However, as she also indicated, this approach has its own contradictions and the tension between the two strategies is often difficult to maintain.

Although all the authors mentioned here have provided valuable evidence to refute earlier ideas about women's passive acceptance of their work in the household and in the labour force and to establish the complicated nature of women's struggles, few have raised the larger theoretical questions about why women resisted, which women resisted, when they formed alliances with men and when they allied with women only, and whether collective or individual action was appropriate.

Along with other theorists, we were challenged by the increasingly evident activities of women and the growing research on women's struggles to deal with some of these issues. In the interviews conducted for *A Working Majority* (1983c), we asked women about their attitudes towards their work. We found that most women, when they submitted, did so not because they believed it was proper, but because they saw few alternatives. We found that most favoured union membership and saw unions as benefitting women, but were critical about the undemocratic structure of unions and their failure to make women's concerns a priority. We found that women often resisted — individually by quitting jobs where they were sexually harassed, for example, or collectively by walking out when faced with hazardous conditions — but frequently put up with bad jobs because they knew there was a large reserve of other women willing to take their places. Our research suggested that women were not simply passive or active, but often both at the same time. However, we did not link these findings to any systematic theory about resistance. Since our research examined only paid jobs, we did not explore resistance related to domestic work. The interviews and research cited above nevertheless led us in some new directions.

Looking Ahead

It seems clear that, as more and more women enter the labour force and as they become less transient there, they will be more likely, both as individuals and as a group, to demand changes not only in the conditions of their paid work but also in those of their domestic and reproductive work. As Marx suggested in reference to men, participation in the labour force brings women together, increases their resources, and changes their consciousness. It also sharpens the contradictions they face.

> Women can see the possibility for control over their reproductive capacities but the control is denied by abortion laws, poor technical development, medical practices and limited information, not to mention the ideology of male superiority. They have 'free choice' in marrying and bearing children, but like the wage worker who is freely compelled to sell labour power, women are compelled by conditions of pregnancy, wage work, medical techniques and legal restrictions to marry and have babies in particular ways. Labour force work interferes with pregnancy and birth; pregnancy and birth interfere with labour force jobs. (Armstrong and Armstrong, 1983b:35-36)

The continuing high unemployment rates for men in many parts of the country, the dramatic growth in the number of lone-parent families headed by women, and the continuing decline in real wages increase women's need for employment income. This pushes them into the labour force, which serves to encourage collective demands. But the process is not that simple. Free trade may mean that women's unemployment rates will rise, forcing many women out of the labour force, isolating them in the home, and putting them into more direct competition with some men and many women for a limited number of jobs, discouraging collective responses. Strategies such as affirmative action, pay equity, and the call for more part-time work may also divide women from each other. The growth in volunteer work may pit woman against woman as well (Armstrong, 1984:130-132; Armstrong and Armstrong, 1989).

The microelectronic technology that is an integral part of the current crisis further threatens to alter the conditions for collective action. Because the new technology has built-in supervisory capacities, because it permits rapid communication over wires of both graphics and the written word, and because it is inexpensive to purchase and operate, it creates the possibility for relocating much of the clerical work now done by women to the household, thus isolating in the home even those women who have paid jobs. The research of Johnson and Johnson (1982) and Lipsig-Mummé (1987) on homework in the garment industry suggests that the movement of wage labour into the home increases the contradictions for women and simultaneously discourages collective action, separating women from each other and increasing their workloads, particularly in terms of domestic tasks. On the other hand, by increasing possibilities for communication and by making the entire system more interconnected and thus more vulnerable, the new technology also opens up the possibility of new forms of resistance.

Meanwhile, developments in reproductive technology, women's increasing labour force participation, collective demands for greater equality, growing threats to male employment, and rising divorce rates have encouraged some women to organize against greater reproductive control for women, against equal pay and job opportunities, and against shared property laws and easier divorce legislation. Citing Dierdre English, Luxton (1982:120) argues that housewives married to working-class and lower-middle-class men may be attracted to such organizations, which allow them "to get out of the family household and become active in the community without denying their traditional housewife role." The same processes that lead some women to become collectively active in demanding greater equality may also lead to collective action designed to reinstate past conditions that promoted the perceived security of subordination and submission.

It is clear that, by all traditional measures, women are better off with a union than without one. Women in unions have better pay, better working conditions, and better job security than non-unionized women, although they often do not fare as well as either unionized or non-unionized men (White, 1980). Perhaps most importantly, unions enhance women's right to say no (Armstrong and Armstrong, 1983c). But, as many have pointed out, unions are usually male-dominated (Briskin and Yanz, 1983; White, 1980). The executives and the bureaucracies are dominated by men; the meetings are often dominated by men and are structured to reflect male concerns as well as male ways of interacting and male time demands. Moreover, unions have been very slow, and often reluctant, to organize in many of the areas where women work.

The various solutions that have been offered for these problems reflect the way the problems have been defined. Some have argued for affirmative action or quota systems to ensure that women have equal representation on the executive. Some have called for a restructuring and rescheduling of meeting times, for daycare provisions, and for an inclusion of what have been called women's concerns on the agenda. Some have organized women's caucuses within unions. Others have rejected the male-dominated union structures altogether and have tried to establish female-dominated unions, especially in areas where unions have been unwilling or unable to organize. All these strategies have helped improve women's position in the workplace and in unions.

What these strategies have demonstrated, however, are the limits of traditional union organizing. Current structures and strategies grew out of a labour process in male-dominated workplaces of the sort that are rapidly disappearing. The earlier shift from craft-based production to industrial production was accompanied by a fundamental shift in the nature of collective organizing, from trade unions to industrial unions. During the transition period, many old strategies that had been appropriate for workers who controlled their tools and techniques lost their usefulness and had to be abandoned in favour of new structures and new methods of organizing based on the connections and relations of the new labour process.

It was during this transition period that women's groups organized outside the workplace in order to improve women's conditions in the labour force. Some women were also struggling within trade union structures but many of the major changes in protective legislation, day-care centres, and standards for women's working conditions resulted primarily from pressure applied by these external groups. Much theoretical work has treated the early women's movement and its more recent version as social movements that ignore women's relationship to the workplace and to unions, although *Feminist Organizing For Change* (Adamson *et al.*, 1988) has begun the exploration of these questions. In the process of women organizing outside the workplace, the lessons that might have been learned about the inadequacies of other organizations involved in workplace change have been lost.

What is needed is some radical thinking about the kinds of workplace organizing that would be appropriate to a new kind of labour process and a new kind of worker. In 1986, 70 percent of Canadian women over fifteen years of age were in the labour force at some time during the year; 68 percent of women fifteen and over had some employment during the year. Women constituted 44 percent of all workers and many women were employed in female-dominated workplaces (Statistics Canada, 1988). Most unionized women work directly or indirectly for the state (Armstrong and Armstrong, 1988). Few women now drop out of the labour force to get married or to have children. Although their labour force participation is still interrupted by "family responsibilities," no longer can we think of women's participation in paid work as transitory. Today, when we speak of a family wage, we are speaking of the income of two people with paid employment. These changes are bound to have fundamental consequences for how people organize and what they organize for.

The flood of women into the labour market is related to changes in the nature of the jobs available. Many of these jobs are in the state sector and involve caring for people, teaching people, or providing people with other forms of assistance or information. More and more of the jobs in the private sector also involve service work. Control over such workers is much different from that exercised on the shop floor. Perhaps most importantly, the structure of such work encourages workers to identify with the goals of employers and of clients, patients, or students. Traditional union strategies such as strikes and slowdowns tend to hurt clients and the long-term working climate of employees. When the employer is the state, strikes save the employer money. These developments suggest that old strategies that harmed the establishment may now be encouraged by employers as a means of saving money or increasing control while delegitimating workers' demands.

Many of the new jobs are in small workplaces, or large workplaces divided into smaller units. Jobs within large organizations are increasingly contracted out to small employers or relocated in dispersed shops. In these workplaces, individuals who would otherwise be called workers are often renamed managers. In some cases, they are made to buy part of the shop and may employ their friends and relatives. Increasingly, work is sent home and the old household shop is reborn, albeit under different conditions. More and more of the work is part-time or short-term. "Retraining" for new jobs is the new form, and the old, large shop is disappearing. These restructuring processes are undermining traditional strategies.

Indeed, these processes have been encouraged both by old union methods of organizing and by new technologies. The very success of union strategies has been a major factor in employers' efforts to decentralize, to divide the work into small packages done by different workers, and to contract it out. The new technologies make it possible to coordinate and control these new structures easily.

Old union structures and old labour laws no longer fit this new reality. Although we can learn a great deal from what have become traditional techniques and although many are still crucial in workplaces organized along old lines, we need to go back to basics. We need to think in terms of new structures, new methods, new demands that reflect this new reality. We also need to recognize that women constitute the dominant labour force in many of these workplaces.

Conclusion

Few theorists would deny that, although strong forces have limited women's possibilities for resistance and have encouraged their submission, women have seldom passively received dictates from their bodies, from men, or from the political economy as a system. Women have been both active and passive, resisting and submitting and creating conditions for further individual and collective responses. But in recovering these past struggles and exposing the complexity of the factors involved, we have developed only tentative suggestions about how, when, and under what conditions women will resist and whether they will do so individually or collectively. And we have done little to link such suggestions to the labour process.

Although feminist theorists agree that women should actively participate in determining their lives, they continue to disagree about whether this action could or should lead to collective or individual demands for collective or individual rights, about where the struggle could or should include men, about whether it could or should involve alterations in or the abolition of the family, about whether it could or should encompass all women. Developments in microelectronic and reproductive technology, as well as the occupational promotion of some women and the growth in part-time and volunteer jobs, threaten to fragment women's work and divide women from each other. New workplaces and new labour processes require new theories and strategies. There is an acute need for a theory that would help us understand not only how women's consciousness develops, but also how different kinds of consciousness arise, and how they lead to different forms of resistance.

Chapter Seven

Women and the State

Introduction

In the current literature, the term state is used to refer not only to those decision-making bodies and bureaucracies normally associated with governments, but also to the judiciary and to those institutions, such as schools, hospitals, daycare centres, and Children's Aid Societies, that are funded by governments. As well, the term refers to the social relations involved in being a citizen of a particular country or territory. Women are employed by the state; they are clients of the state; they are regulated by the state; they have (or lack) services provided by the state; they appeal to the state for protection and redress. The dominant ideology and women's ideas about themselves are influenced by the ideas perpetuated in state institutions, by the organization of state structures and services, by the structure of state policies and practices.

Moreover, the state has a profound influence on what is deemed private and what is deemed public. First, within the formal economy, the state determines what constitutes the public sector, what constitutes the private sector, and to what extent the private sector is governed by public regulations. Second, the state helps structure what falls into the public realm of state and formal economy, and what belongs to the private realm of household and family, as well as the extent to which the latter is governed by public regulations (Armstrong and Armstrong, 1988). Not surprisingly, then, feminists have become increasingly concerned with theorizing the state.

As is the case in other areas, feminists have held differing perspectives on how the state is to be understood. Those working from a radical feminist perspective have emphasized the state's role in reproducing male dominance and thus have frequently advocated establishing alternatives to state structures and practices instead of appealing to the state. Those who focused on ideas and who have been categorized as liberal feminists tended to see the state as basically neutral, as a place to go for protection, services, regulations, and redress. Like the radical feminists, those beginning from a historical materialist perspective rejected the notion of the state's neutrality and stressed the state's role in reproducing unequal social relations. However, they also focused attention on the state's role in encouraging the conditions for profit-making. Dorothy Smith (1977:25) for example, argued that "it becomes increasingly clear to us that the state is not on our side, that the state is not evenhanded with respect to women any more than it is evenhanded with respect to the demands of the working class." As Melanie Randall (1988:10) explained in her review of state theories, "one of the key questions for a specifically feminist approach to the state is the extent to which the state is autonomous from, or is itself one of, the structures and relations of male dominance."

In spite of these differences, however, feminists of all persuasions have been pushed by the very pervasiveness of the state to interact with and make demands on state organizations and legislatures. Whatever their theoretical perspective, feminists made submissions to the Royal Commission on the Status of Women. A wide variety of feminists has spoken out on issues such as equal pay legislation and sexual harassment in the workplace, rape, and property rights. Whatever their theoretical approach, feminists have come together to make demands on the state regarding an extensive range of issues. The work connected to organizing to address these issues has brought not only the women but also their theories on the state closer together. So has their experience with state reaction to their demands and with state policies and programs.

Fewer and fewer feminists would argue that the state basically acts in a neutral way, as arbitrator of competing demands. At the same time, however, more and more feminists have come to realize that the state is not simply an instrument of class or male rule; that it can indeed work for the benefit of at least some women. Feminists who hold many different perspectives have come to see the complexity of the state and come to appreciate that it may have very contradictory effects for women; sometimes serving women's short-term interests while reducing their long-term gains; sometimes dividing women from each other and at other times bringing women together. All would agree that the state must be understood in a sex-conscious way; that all state action and inaction has a different impact on women than on men, and often varying effects on women from diverse classes, races, and ethnic groups.

The State and Women's Employment

Our examination of women employed directly and indirectly by the state led us to develop an outline that began with the state's interest in creating the conditions for profit growth. But we did not understand the state simply, or even primarily, as a pawn of capitalists' interests, because we saw the state responding to workers' demands and to different demands made by a variety of employers. As well, we emphasized the state's role in manipulating the separation of private and public, and saw these strategies as having sex-specific results.

As we explained in "Taking Women Into Account" (Armstrong and Armstrong, 1988) in the postwar period, Keynesian theory provided a coherent justification of, and a guide for, a Canadian state already deeply involved in the economy, and for a government concerned about preventing a repetition of the revolts and the depression that had followed the previous world war. A clear commitment to full employment was defined in Keynesian terms — jobs that would pay enough "to satisfy the immediate primary needs of a man and his family" (Keynes, 1936:97). Two explicit strategies designed to attain full employment were developed. On the one hand, capital would be assisted through the development of the infrastructure and through direct and indirect financial support to business. On the other hand, demand would be sustained through both employment-related schemes such as unemployment insurance and universal programs such as family allowances. Because most employees were male, employment-related schemes applied mainly to men and served to tie them into the labour force and to reinforce their position as primary breadwinners for households. Even today, the large number of women in the labour force receive significantly less than men from Unemployment Insurance and Workers' Compensation (Armstrong, 1984). This disparity reflects the principles built into these programs. Because most of those who received family allowances and other subsidies such as Family Benefits were women, these schemes served to tie women more firmly into the household, encouraging their dependency and making full labour force participation more difficult for married women. The state explicitly set out to reinforce women's dependency and male financial responsibility in the postwar years as a means of maintaining stability and full employment firmly relegating most married women to the private sphere.

Large corporations enjoyed rising profits in these years and faced strong male unions in their capital-intensive industries. Unlike smaller owners who could draw on large reserves of mainly non-unionized and often immigrant female labour, and who could easily run away to other territories when labour demands became too strong, these corporations tended to look favourably on what we have called the socialization of the social wage. That is, they supported the idea of taxing everyone to provide for such schemes as health care and family allowance as a means of avoiding the demands on them made by their increasingly powerful workers. The rapidly expanding welfare state meant, as John Calvert (1984) and others have demonstrated, a redistribution of resources from employed males to some unemployed males and to many women. And it served to reinforce women's dependency on men and on the state. But it also served in contradictory fashion to provide more jobs for women in the public sphere. Women constitute the majority of the workers in education and health as well as a high proportion of those working in public administration and in other services provided by the state (Armstrong, 1984:Chapter 4). The dramatic rise in state employment took place during a period of relatively full employment for men. Women were available and women were thought to have the appropriate skills. Brought together in large state institutions, many women formed unions, and the right to maintain their jobs after marriage, to name only a few. Various studies showed that women's incomes relative to men's were lowest in the competitive sector and highest in the private sector (Denton and Hunter, 1984:36); that "almost 60 percent of all female pension plan members were in the public sector in 1974" (Collins, 1978:63), and that women were more likely to become managers and to achieve a measure of job security if they worked directly or indirectly for the state (Armstrong, 1984). These victories also helped reduce the turnover in the female labour force, which further increased the possibilities for union organizing. "In 1981, the majority of women who belonged to unions were paid directly by the governments" (Armstrong, 1984:129).

Unlike many businesses in the private sector, the state could not threaten to run away and relocate in another country if workers resisted. The fact that it had few alternative sources of labour strengthened women's unions in the state sector. Public and corporate support for state services, along with relatively full government coffers, also contributed to the state's acquiescence to workers' demands. Concerned with legitimacy, the state responded to demands to provide more individual and collective rights for women. Federal and provincial governments established women's divisions within their bureaucracies and often appointed women to head them. Even women outside the state sector benefited from the growing strength of unions and from the women's movement. The state set an example for other workers. It introduced regulations on equal pay, and minimum standards in the workplace.

The expansion of services relieved some of women's domestic burdens at the same time that women were acquiring jobs performing these services for pay in the market. It should be noted, however, that many of these services were newly developed and had never been, nor could they easily be, provided in individual private households. Many people in hospitals and homes for the aged, for example, could not be cared for in the home because they were receiving treatments that involved new medical technologies and procedures. In other words, a significant proportion of these services could not be "sent home," as many conservatives have suggested they should be.

The expansion of the public sector in the formal economy, then, contributed to the legitimation of women's collective rights and to women's individual rights while reducing demands on the household and somewhat limiting public involvement in the private (household) sphere. Women's possibilities for seeking paid employment increased.

All these developments suggested that the state was on the side of women; that rational appeals to equity would transform state practices in relation to women. But, in spite of these well publicized gains, the state was not a model employer for women. In her study of the federal civil service, Kathleen Archibald (1970:44) found that women were concentrated in the lowest paid jobs and within a few occupations. Although women in the public sector had a better chance of becoming managers than those in private companies, Archibald's investigation indicated that most "women do not initiate such action for men in the Government offices and they do not initiate much for women either." Such practices suggested to many theorists that the state was responding more to women's collective strength than to a rational argument for equity, and that the state was more concerned with the appearance of equity than with treating women fairly.

Theorists were also suspicious about the various women's bureaus and organizations set up within state bureaucracies and about those established with state funds. During the 1970s, Esther Clark Wright

(1977) had started with the assumption that the state was at least neutral and argued that women should enter state organizations in order to shape policies and programs in women's interests. A decade later, however, Sue Findlay (1985, 1987, 1988) was using her experiences as head of a state bureau charged with addressing women's issues to argue that the structures provided only the appearance of responding to women's concerns. These bureaus, she maintained, failed to produce substantive changes for women precisely because the state is not neutral, because "the resistance of a male-dominated state to women's equality, together with its reluctance to intervene in the private sector to enforce proportional representation, has severely limited progress" (Findlay, 1985:33). Progress was also limited by the women's movement's failure "to offer many concrete proposals to the state" (Findlay, 1988:6). Feminists in the bureaucracy were torn between their responsibilities to their employers and their commitment to feminist principles.

Others (Barnsley, 1988; Maroney, 1988; Smith, 1986) have suggested that the structure of state enterprises and the practices women must follow in order to be eligible for state funding in non-state organizations transform the projects and take them out of women's hands. Projects initiated by feminists often found it impossible to survive without state funds. However, the processes of applying for funds and of conforming to regulations distracted women from the task at hand and often fundamentally altered their plans, especially if some workers in these organizations became dependent on state financing for their jobs. Furthermore, state funding often created differences among the women working in these feminist organizations, as a result of high, state-determined salaries going to some and no salaries going to others.

New developments in the 1980s led to new critiques of the state. From the late 1960s on, conditions in the market began to deteriorate. Large corporations in the primary and secondary sectors began facing falling profits. Their equipment was aging and, as a result, other countries offered an increasingly attractive labour force because new plants, if required, could be located virtually anywhere. Male unemployment rose and union strength declined. Fewer and fewer households could rely entirely on the man's wage. Under such conditions, large corporations looked less favourably on the social wage (Armstrong and Armstrong, 1988).

Smaller employers in the growing service sector relied primarily on a non-unionized female labour force. The large reserve of women searching for paid employment meant that these employers could actively oppose state regulations, the social wage, and the steady growth of unionization among women. At the same time, the increasing un-ionization of women made some of these employers more and more concerned about their labour supply. There was growing pressure on the state to cut back on state services and regulations and to discipline its workers, to set another kind of example.

In a declining economy, the state was able, to some extent, to col-lapse its legitimation and accumulation functions. What has become the primary legitimate function is accumulation, although it should be noted that there are real limits to this process. The top priorities are a level playing field, a free-market economy, and a balanced budget. Nevertheless, the state has discovered that some programs, such as pension plans, cannot be abandoned.

There has been a significant shift in distinctions between the public and private sectors as the state deregulates the formal economy, reduces the state sector, and increasingly regulates private households. With large reserves of both female and male labour and with more support for reductions in state expenditures, the state has been able to use its not inconsiderable power to discipline workers and simul-taneously blame them for deterioration in services while saving money during state-sector workers' strikes. Workers have been legislated back to work by their state-sector employers and the budgets of state-funded organizations have been reduced. Because more than half of all un-ionized women are employed in the state sector, such legislation has profound implications for women's future choices and working con-ditions.

In line with this new market philosophy, capitalist management prin-ciples have been applied to state-sector workers, intensifying the work of these employees, most of whom are women, and increasing the female labour reserve. Many of the gains made in job security, rela-tive pay, and working conditions have been undermined. The cut-backs in state services, together with new management strategies, are reducing the number of jobs and the number of hours of paid em-ployment, especially for women. Privatization has forced women into less secure employment under worse conditions. More and more wom-en provide a part-time reserve army that permits labour intensifica-tion and a reduction of the social wage (Armstrong and Armstrong, 1988). And, in spite of some significant changes, most women in the state sector still do women's work at women's wages (Armstrong, 1984).

But women have not passively accepted these developments; the state has not simply had things its own way. Nurses in particular have collectively gone on strike, sometimes illegally, and have individually walked away from nursing, creating the "nursing shortage."

During the same period, women won the inclusion of women's rights in the new Constitution and, with this victory, increased their involvement as employees and as policy makers in the state. The results, as Findlay (1988) has pointed out, have been contradictory both for the women who work in the state sector and for the women's movement. Feminist resources have been diverted from other areas. Although feminists are increasingly seeing the "limits imposed by state agendas," they are forced to respond to state proposals. In the process, Findlay (1988:7-8) has argued, the government "has institutionalized the representation of women's issues in the 'unequal' structure of representation that is the basis of policy-making. It now has the capacity, and uses it, to redefine our issues and shape our strategies."

As more and more women have become employees of the state — either in traditional women's jobs or in newly created jobs related to women's issues — feminists have become more and more aware of the need to theorize this aspect of the state and to transform old explanations. What has emerged is a picture of the state that reveals it as complex, dynamic, and contradictory. The state has not been a neutral employer. Nor has it been clearly on the side of women. But it has not simply been an employer like the rest, responding primarily to capitalists' demands. The state has, at times, responded to the demands of women workers, thus retaining both its legitimacy and its employees. Some state policy makers have been committed to, and have worked for, women's issues. As a result, women have found many of their best jobs in the state sector and many women are in a better position working for the state than they are working in the private sector. Yet employment in the state bureaucracy is loaded with contradictions for women, especially for women working on what are defined as women's issues. Furthermore, many of women's gains are currently being undermined. We are far from having an adequate theory to explain these contradictory and complex practices, but we do have a useful beginning.

State Policies and Regulations

The state not only provides jobs for women. It also regulates or fails to regulate women's work in the home and in the market. Moreover, state policies can have a profound impact on the nature and conditions of women's work in both spheres. Such regulations and policies influence whether or not women take paid work, where that paid work in done, and under what conditions work within and outside of the home is undertaken.

In the formal economy, regulations related to maternity leave, equal pay, and sexual harassment have long been considered women's issues. But, given the segregation of the market, regulations and policies related to such matters as minimum wage, union organizing, hours of work, pensions, and health and safety have different effects on women than on men, and thus become women's issues (Armstrong and Armstrong, 1982; Cameron, 1984; Dulude, 1978; Cornish and Ritchie, 1980; White, 1983).

Moreover, the state's influence on women's work is not limited to regulations and policies developed for the market. As Allan Moscovitch (1983:vi-vii) has pointed out in the introduction to his bibliography on the Canadian state,

> Social welfare has been concerned with regulating the biological and social reproduction of the family. The importance of legal limitations on sexuality such as laws relating to consent, marriage, divorce, contraception, and abortion can too easily be overlooked when social welfare is only considered to be expressed in state expenditures. Such regulations are relatively costless but of key importance to understanding the nature of the welfare state.

Such laws, it should be added, are also of crucial importance to understanding the nature of women's work within and outside the home. According to Wally Seccombe (1986:25),

> the social control of women is *centered* upon their reproductive capacities in a vast range of societies. If this generalization is valid, ... there are compelling feminist reasons for paying close attention to the demographic regulators of women's fertility and to their change over time.

Seccombe went on to say that "little progress has been made on fertility" (1986:25). Much of this social regulation involves state legislation or programs, and therefore requires a theory of the state.

Although more feminist analysis of the social regulation is required, there has been some investigation of the different effects on men and on women of state policies that influence work in the home and in the underground economy. As is the case in the formal economy, some policies and regulations related to the household are unquestionably women's issues. A number of feminists have drawn out the particular implications for women of state policies and regulations in such areas as childcare, divorce, marital property rights, prostitution, abortion, and contraception (Ambert, 1980; Bell, 1987; Bouma and Bouma, 1975; Dulude, 1984; Eichler, 1983; Guberman and Wolfe, 1985; Johnson and Dineen, 1981; MacLeod, 1980; McLaren and McLaren, 1986; Shaver, 1985-86). Given the segregation of many women in the home and their responsibilities for childrearing as well as for childbearing, regulations and policies related to such matters as housing, welfare programs, transportation, paid work done at home, and immigration have also increasingly been defined by feminists as women's issues (Baxter, 1988; Carty and Brand, 1988; McClain and Doyle, 1983; Ng, 1986; Storrie, 1987; Wallis et al., 1988; Warren, 1986).

Feminists have agreed that the state has a different impact on women than on men, but there has been less agreement on the desirability and the consequences of state regulations and policies for women. Liberal reformers in particular have seen the state as a means of protecting women from the worst excesses of capitalist development and male privilege. As Caroline Andrew (1984:670) has pointed out, "women's organizing and women's organizations are crucial to the developments" culminating in the modern Canadian welfare state. Feminists have demanded, and won, protective legislation for women and children in the labour force, maternity leave and equal pay legislation, state policies on sexual harassment and marital property rights, and changes in the legislation on abortion and contraception.

Not all feminists have been equally enthusiastic about these victories, however. Some have argued that the results of these struggles were at best contradictory, often serving in the long run to reinforce both women's subordination and the inequalities among women. For example, the struggle for protective legislation in the late nineteenth and early twentieth centuries was based on biological assumptions about women's special capacities, which tended either to lump women together with children, or to emphasize their special health needs (Ursel, 1986:163). Fought for primarily by women of privilege, legislation that protected women from some working conditions and that allowed women into some "womanly" professions encouraged the segregation of most women into the least desirable jobs at low wages while permitting some women to work in jobs that had professional status and utilized women's "special capabilities" (Kealey, 1979:9). In her analysis of this reform period, Jane Ursel (1986:158) concluded that "the liberalization of family law, the emergence of women's and children's rights, while appearing as the end of patriarchy, are in fact, a manifestation of the growth of social patriarchy." Ursel maintained that "in the social patriarchal mode, the power and authority to control women's access to resources is increasingly vested in the state through the promulgation of labour, welfare and family law" (155), and that "thus an important aspect of labour legislation is the role it plays in perpetuating the sexual division of labour, maintaining women's role as primarily reproductive and reinforcing patriarchal structures by effectively restricting women's productive role" (161-162).

Similar discussions have taken place regarding the much more recent struggle for equal pay legislation (Armstrong *et al.*, 1988; Armstrong and Armstrong, 1989; Lewis, 1988; Mitchell, 1988; Warskett, 1988). The first versions of equal pay legislation applied to identical or substantially identical work done for the same employer and required an aggrieved employee to initiate complaints. Maximum penalties were low and some employees were excluded from even these limited provisions. Such legislation was based on the assumption that pay inequality was a minor and individual problem for a few female employees who were discriminated against by a few misguided employers who had been socialized into an inappropriate value system. Given that women and men tended to work in different jobs and often for different employers, and given that the complaints-based procedures was both costly and risky, few women saw wage gains under this legislation. The legislation gave legitimacy to a state that formally required equality based on individual rights, while denying most women pay equivalent to that of men. Lorraine Mitchell (1988:64) has argued that

> The basic problem with most of these measures lies in their failure to recognize that women's oppression is endemic to our system. Men benefit from wage discrimination. Women's lack of economic independence means they remain trapped in abusive relationships with individual men and powerless in a society controlled by men. And lower wages mean higher profits. Yet all legislative measures to end wage discrimination are based on the assumption that the society we live in is equitable and just, and that the injustice done to women can be addressed by minor tinkerings with this system.

But not all those who have appealed to the state for redress on this issue have assumed that the state is a neutral arbitrator or that wage inequalities result from individual inadequacies. The Ontario Equal Pay Coalition — a feminist lobby that brought together women from unions, professional organizations, and community groups — won legislation that began with the explicit assumption that there was systemic discrimination and that employers in both the private and the public sectors had to be forced to develop plans to counteract this systemic discrimination. Under the Ontario Pay Equity Act, men's and women's jobs must be compared on the basis of skill, effort, responsibilities, and working conditions, not on the basis of identical content.

Although this legislation represents a significant improvement over earlier versions, it still reflects the contradictory role of the state and some inappropriate assumptions about women's work. Central to the legislation is the requirement that jobs be evaluated in a manner free of gender bias so that men's and women's jobs can be compared on the basis of their value. As some feminists (Armstrong and Armstrong, 1989; Lewis, 1988; Warskett, 1988) have pointed out, this requirement ignores the fact that value is primarily determined by power, not by job content. The need for job evaluations can reduce struggles over pay "to technical procedures controlled by 'the experts' and subject to manipulation by employers and the state" (Lewis, 1988:127). As Findlay (1988) argued in the case of other women's issues, a political process may be transformed into a bureaucratic one defined by the state. Moreover, the introduction of very detailed job evaluation schemes designed to capture women's extensive skills and responsibilities may increase the power of employers and change the minimum requirements of the job (Armstrong and Armstrong, 1989). And, finally, the technical details of the legislation make it difficult for many women to understand, limit the impact of the Act, and mean that some women will benefit and many will not. As a result, differences among women may increase and the strength of their unions may be undermined. Immigrant women in particular are unlikely to benefit from the legislation. Nevertheless, the contradiction between the promise and the reality of the Act, as well as the struggles arising from its implementation, may increase women's strength and enhance their understanding of the state.

Although many feminists have argued that state legislation and policies have not produced substantial changes for women and that what appear to be gains often constitute new forms of subordination, it seems clear that in some areas, at least some women are better off with the legislation than without it. As is the case with employment in the public sector, the consequences are contradictory and vary among women. Reflecting on women's experiences with equal pay legislation, Rosemary Warskett (1988:69) concluded that "more theory building is necessary to explain the ways in which both gender and class inequality are reproduced and supported by the state within liberal democratic societies in general and Canadian society in particular."

The State and Ideology

The state, through the education system, through the media, through regulations and social policies, through the very structure of its organizations, and through the law, reinforces the dominant ideology. Mary O'Brien (1984) suggests that Gramsci provides some important clues to understanding the role of the state in maintaining acceptable knowledge or, in Gramsci's terms, common sense.

> Ideology is not a product of naked coercion but of social practice in the realm of everyday life and thought, where consciousness acts on the experiential social context in which the subject is immersed, and where men (sic) can only deal with the realities that history presents to them. (1984:88)

There is no simple division between a material base and an ideological superstructure; although the state works to protect the hegemony of the ruling class, the results are often contradictory. "Hegemony is the 'motor' of common sense, defining reality and organizing consent to such ruling class definitions of truth, but in the very process it creates the possibility of counter-hegemony" (89).

And, we would add, hegemony is maintained through compromises in which some demands of the subordinate classes and sex are met, and through the constant reproduction of institutions, social relations, and ideas that provide the basis for consent. Varda Burstyn (1983), for example, has shown that the structure of state bureaucracies promotes men who are aggressive, verbal, and decisive but negatively judges women who behave this way. Similarly, Action travail des femmes argued, in charging Canadian National (a huge federal crown corporation involved in the railway, steamship, telecommunications, and hotel businesses) with discrimination before the Canadian Human Rights Commission (Canadian National Railway Co. and Canadian Human Rights Commission, 1983), that it was the structure of the corporation as much as specific practices that excluded women.

Beyond documenting the images projected in schools and in the media, few theorists have explored the implications of the state's role in the reproduction of common sense and its consequences for women. Heather Jon Maroney has recently begun this process. She argued that there has been a shift in political discourse to include both the masculine and the feminine, that women have been able to constitute themselves as a political force, and that there has been a shift "in the state toward egalitarianism in its legal constitution of gender relations." In other words, there has been a change both in common sense and in the structures that reproduce gender relations.

> In sum, we can say that the importance of all of these shifts is not just that gender relations have become an important axis of politics and ideology, but also that a new relationship between gender politics and the politico-ideological field as a whole has been established (Maroney, 1988:27).

Influenced by such arguments, we began exploring how state structures work to reproduce and challenge the common sense of male and ruling class hegemony within the context of a state hospital. Indeed, it was primarily as a result of our earlier work on the impact of the economic crisis on women and our current study of the effects of state cutbacks on female hospital workers that we became concerned about theorizing the relationship of women to the state. The services provided by the hospital both benefited and confined women. The available work provided many rewards but simultaneously exerted enormous pressures on women in their work at home as well as in the labour force. Changes resulting from cutbacks both improved and worsened working conditions and patient care, both in the hospital and in the household. Union victories had both negative and positive consequences for women's work. The state as employer acted like and unlike employers in the private sector, with contradictory consequences for women. In general, the hospital functioned in a way that reflected the interests of those in power, but it also provided important benefits for, and represented some demands made by, other groups. These very structures and practices were simultaneously reinforcing and altering "common sense" understandings of women's place.

More recently, we have suggested that state legislation can also play an important role in challenging "common sense" (Armstrong and Armstrong, 1989). In the case of the Ontario Pay Equity Act, for example, the state has recognized systemic discrimination and has legitimated demands for equal pay. Although the implementation of the Act will not result in equal pay for women, it may transform what is acceptable in terms of pay differences and provide a justification for women's continuing demands.

Here, too, feminists have increasingly seen the role of the state as contradictory, even though it often reinforces an ideology that relegates women to a secondary status.

The State and Services

This ideology is reflected in and reinforced by the services the state provides for women. Women constitute the majority of state clients in many areas. The redistribution of resources that takes place within the welfare state is primarily from the employed to the unemployed, from the young to the old, from those without children to those with young people living at home. Since women are the majority of those without paid employment, of the old, and of those with responsibility for young children, the redistribution tends to flow from men to women. The majority of those using health care services are women, and female students now outnumber their male counterparts even at the university level. Such services, and their distribution, have a profound effect on determining which women can, or must, enter the labour force.

State policies on services determine where women provide services and whether or not women are paid for the provision of services. States can, and are, returning many of these services to women in the home (Armstrong, 1984). In light of their responsibility for the young, the old, the sick, and the disabled, women have fewer employment possibilities. If the private household is a pivotal location of women's subordination in Canadian society, then state interventions vis-à-vis women have long had, and continue to have, the contradictory effects of breaking down and simultaneously reinforcing the public/private dichotomy.

This is evident, for example, in state services related to welfare. On the one hand, welfare legislation has served to reinforce women's responsibility for children and their dependency on the state. On the other hand, as Patricia Evans and Eilene McIntyre (1987) have pointed out, the recent tendency to move women from welfare to work has undermined women's right to income maintenance and reduced their chances of keeping their families together and of spending time with their children. At the same time, lack of complementary services and lack of sufficient access to educational programs ensure that most women are locked into the lowest-level jobs at wages insufficient to support a family.

Several feminists have analyzed the "mixed blessing" of state services for women. Roxanna Ng (1986), for example, has exposed how the structure of employment services for immigrant women ensures that these women remained segregated in the lowest-level jobs and dependent on their families. The articles on health care brought together by Kathleen McDonnell (1986) in *Adverse Effects* suggest that the provision of health care services limits women's possibilities for controlling their own bodies. And Susan Russell (1986) has shown how practices inherent in our educational system encourage a sexual division of labour. Although these feminists have illustrated the negative consequences of these services for women, it is clear from their research that women need these services and that some women benefit from them.

Radical feminists in particular have argued that the way out of this contradictory position of wanting state services but rejecting their consequences is to establish independent services run by women. However, the need for funding and for relations with the rest of the population often transform these services into structures very similar to those provided directly by the state.

Although feminists have exposed the tendency of state services to reinforce existing power relations and ideologies, they have not developed an adequate theory to explain the nature of state services. Nor have they come up with strategies that adequately address their concerns.

Conclusion

As is the case in other areas of theory, there has been both continuing debate about, and some convergence on, central issues. Few theorists would now view the state as either a neutral arbitrator or the instrument of class rule, as simply benefiting or harming women. Most would agree that the state has a profound, and contradictory, influence on women's work. Most would agree with Jenson (1986:41) that the contribution of the state "is variable not only across social formations but across time," and with Mahon (1977:193) that state activities "reflect inter- and intra-class contradictions — contradictions which are likely to be 'resolved' in such a manner that the 'general political interest' of the power bloc is maintained." As a result, the state has simultaneously contributed to women's liberation and to their subordination. It is indeed a contested terrain (Armstrong and Armstrong, 1988; Mahon, 1977). But there is little agreement on how the state is to be understood or addressed, and we are a long way from a coherent feminist theory of the state.

In a period of retreat from the welfare state, such theory is crucial in determining strategy. If the state is neither simply beneficial nor simply harmful, under what conditions do we demand the maintenance of state services, support their elimination, or fight for their transformation? Regardless of which option we favour, we must ask which women will benefit, and how our demands will affect work in the home and in the labour force, the relationship between these two kinds of work, and women's relationship to men. Finally, how can we go about getting what we want? Only with systematic theory can we begin to deal adequately with these questions.

Chapter Eight

Feminist Methodology

Introduction

From the beginning of the current wave of feminism, questions about what should be studied, how it should be studied, and how theory should be related to empirical research have been central. These questions are still crucial issues in feminist debates.

The Subject

As Dorothy Smith (1974) forcefully argued, women have often been invisible in the social science literature. But as Meg Luxton (1984:61) has more recently pointed out, social science has not ignored women, but rather it has treated them in ways that fail to make them the subjects of history. Male criteria were assumed to be universal criteria in what Mary O'Brien (1976) called "malestream thought." "Women's oppression is qualitatively different from class oppression, and the qualitative differentiation which must be made in the first instance in theoretical terms simply does not emerge from Marx's work in a direct way" (O'Brien, 1979:100). In addition, what Margrit Eichler (1980) called the double standard meant that identical behaviour was differently evaluated according to whether it was exhibited by women or by men.

In her introduction to *The Effects of Feminist Approaches on Research Methodologies*, Winnie Tomm (1989:2) has offered a concise summary of the feminist critique:

> The so-called objectivity of male defined rationality was found
> to be replete with unexamined pervasive prejudice against wom-
> en's interests, especially with regard to academic research. The
> topics were defined by male interests, the methods used to il-
> luminate the topics were devised by men, the messages commu-
> nicated to the public were those which reflected the interests of
> the powerful who were usually men.

Research reflecting feminist perspectives was seldom funded. Even
when feminists managed to conduct their research, it was unlikely
to be published in the traditional academic outlets. New strategies were
required (Andrew, 1989).

In response to such criticisms and to pressures from feminists, mainstream books about families, about work, and about inequality began
to include chapters on women. Journals were pushed to publish the
odd article on women. However, the dominant texts continued to assume a sexless universal person — a person whose likeness was more
male than female — and the chapters on women were confined to narrowly defined "women's issues." Today, we still get unemployment
figures and female unemployment figures, a chapter on workers and
then one on female workers, as if there were a norm and then an aber-
ration. Within the more radical political economy publications, the
materialist analysis of women's subordination ran parallel to, but seldom integrated with, other theoretical developments. Women, and
a few men, were left to deal with that stuff. Here, too, women's work
was relegated to a secondary position outside the main task of theorizing production.

Increasingly, women become a more prominent category, integrated in the text. In the manner of Canadian versions of American texts,
however, publications devoted to examining women all too often merely inserted women in place of men, without transforming the concepts to make them sex-conscious. All too frequently, sex was simply
added in, as one more variable among many. Alternatively, as Ruth
Pierson and Alison Prentice (1982:110) observed of historical writing,
authors assigned "importance to women only insofar as they have
contributed to or supplemented the work or achievements of men."

These strategies for including women reflected the definition of what
constituted a women's issue. The earliest writing of both historical
materialists and radical feminists viewed the subordination of women
as embedded in the entire fabric of society, although one group iden-

tified production and the other human reproduction as the primary basis for this subordination. Marlene Dixon (1972:230), for example, argued that "class and property relations are the source of the oppression of women," whereas Jane Likely (1972:158-159) insisted that "women's liberation demands that liberation pre-empt revolution." For theorists from both perspectives, the subject matter of feminist theory was the organization of the social structure. It was not restricted to some finite, clearly demarcated area of women's issues, as it had been in early liberal feminist theory. Materialist and radical arguments implied that women's subordination had to be central to all social theory and research, that all questions were women's questions.

As research has increasingly exposed the pervasiveness of segregation and subordination, and as more women have entered and become vocal in the public sphere, it has become more and more difficult for theorists concerned with the position of women to restrict their focus to a narrow range of women's issues. Here feminists from all persuasions, including liberal feminists, have tended to converge.

A key recommendation of the Royal Commission on the Status of Women (Canada, 1970) illustrates this development (see Armstrong and Armstrong, 1982). When the Royal Commission recommended the establishment of a council to "advise on matters pertaining to women," the objective seemed clear. "We want for women no special status, only equal status; no separate realm, only full acceptance in the present human world" (1970:390). However, as the resulting Canadian Advisory Council on the Status of Women conducted research, responded to feminists' demands, and evaluated state programs, equal status was revealed as a complex and difficult goal. And the definition of "matters pertaining to women" expanded enormously. It quickly became clear that women would have to be treated differently in many circumstances if they were not to suffer from their sex. As Judge Rosalie Abella would later explain in her Royal Commission report *Equality in Employment* (Canada, 1984:3), "to treat everyone the same may be to offend the notion of equality. Ignoring differences may mean ignoring legitimate needs." Each time a particular area was investigated, it became clear that it could not be separated from the entire organization of the social structure. It became clear that all questions were women's questions.

For us, this kind of progression meant rethinking theory, and involved us in yet another debate about the appropriate level of analysis for the theorization of gender. We argued that, in materialist analysis, to insist on distinguishing a highest level of abstraction that entirely excludes consideration of a sexual division of labour is to be sexist — to reinforce the notion of women being hidden from history, or more accurately, from theory. It is also to guarantee an inadequate understanding of capitalism, given that the split between the public and the private, and thus a sexual division of labour, is essential to this mode of production, at the highest level of abstraction. (Armstrong and Armstrong, 1983b:28)

Patricia Connelly (1983:57-58) has rejected this argument, agreeing with Wally Seccombe that there is a "sexless and epochal abstraction of the capitalist mode of production" and that it is at the level of the social formation that "the relations of production intersect, combine and conflict with the relations of gender in different classes and in different historical periods within one society, and in different societies." The issue remains a central one because its theoretical and political implications are significant. We contend that our position implies that the subordination of women's work cannot be completely eliminated under capitalism, and that it will be eliminated under whatever succeeds capitalism only if the different reproductive capacities of women and men are adequately taken into account.

Method

The emphasis on the techniques used in and the legitimacy given to the so-called "hard" data of quantitative analysis ran counter to the "personal is political" assumption at the core of feminist thinking. In her introduction to the first edition of *Women in Canada*, Marylee Stephenson (1973:xv) explained that, in the women's movement, "every woman's life experience provides valid information about certain aspects of women's situation in general." Although she then offered the qualification that such information provides "a valuable resource area outside the strictly academic field," this observation became increasingly outdated as more and more feminist research focused on recording women's daily lives.

Whatever feminists' position on the appropriate level of analysis, most would agree that all issues are women's issues. Women must be acknowledged as subjects different from men, making all research a concern for women. This means rethinking categories and approaches, not just "fitting women in."

Like dual systems theorists who developed new approaches to human reproduction but left old theories of production virtually untouched (Armstrong, 1984:36-38), researchers who relied on interviews, diaries, personal reminiscences, and group discussions as a means of examining women's work left statistical analytical techniques untransformed.

Those who argued for the exclusive use of qualitative techniques maintained that quantitative techniques both failed to capture many aspects of women's lives and objectified women. As these feminists worked with qualitative techniques and transformed them into what was increasingly called a feminist methodology, they also developed a more thorough critique of old approaches, both qualitative and quantitative. They rejected the idea of researchers who stood "outside" the work being studied and who assumed that they knew more than those actually doing the work. They rejected the tendency to fit women into preconceived categories or theories. And they rejected the pretense as well as the ideal of "value-free" research. They sought to develop, as Thelma McCormack (1989:15) has so cogently explained,

A new kind of knowledge which did not attempt to be objective, and was no longer attempting to 'predict and control', knowledge without social causation and without looking for regularities that might lead to 'laws', would obliterate the line between subject and object and create both a richer knowledge and a more ethical one. Knowledge would be consciousness-raising for both the people who carried out the studies and those who were studied.

Many of those who argued for this approach held that research on women could only be done by women, because research required not only a commitment to feminist principles and an empathy with those who were studied, but also a shared history. Some argued that this meant that only immigrants could study immigrants, and only people of colour could study people of colour.

Many of the materialists and liberal feminists examining women's work had tended to rely on traditional social science techniques to analyze quantitative data, establishing the segregation of the labour market with these tools. Radical feminists in particular, however, preferred qualitative approaches to the investigation of the commonalities of women's work, establishing women's shared experiences, particularly in the work of mothering and in relations with men. Indeed, as McCormack (1981) pointed out, many feminists rejected the whole notion of scientific investigation, arguing that the rationality it assumed reflected a male way of thinking. They argued instead for collections of women's personal experiences, letting women speak for themselves.

It was important to emphasize that women often had a very clear understanding of their situation; that they frequently understood more than researchers. Moreover, it was important to recognize that how women understood the world and their place in it had an important impact on their behaviour and relations. However, many of those making these arguments seemed to suggest that the woman recording women's experiences was objective and value free — a mere cipher. Yet this was precisely what they had accused male researchers of doing with their "objective" research. These female researchers still selected the lives to be recorded and the parts of lives to be reported. Equally important, the presentation of researcher as recorder denied what was at the core of feminism — the connecting of the personal and the political and the commitment to change. These connections required theoretical assumptions and an articulated framework, not an invisible researcher. As Linda Briskin (1989:91) has pointed out,

> An anti-theory emphasis on personal experience can individualize difference (each experience as unique) to such a degree that the deep-rooted processes by which experience is socially constructed are concealed. As a result, the complex patterning of women's experiences of class, race, gender, and sexual orientation is masked; even the interconnectedness between different aspects of an individual woman's experience (for example, the links between household and workplace), can be made less accessible, thus exacerbating the fragmentation of everyday life within patriarchal capitalism.

In our early work (Armstrong and Armstrong, 1975), we used quantitative data to investigate women's paid employment. As is the case with many other feminist researchers, our purpose was political. We wanted to use evidence that would be both academically acceptable as rigorous research and readily comprehensible to a wide audience. We developed two measures of segregation to explore the changes over time in the allocation of jobs to women and to men. The degree of sex-typing — the proportion of jobs that go to women — was measured by calculating the percentage of all workers in an industry or occupation who were women. The degree of concentration — the proportion of all women who worked in a particular industry or occupation — was measured by calculating the percentage of female workers employed in an industry or occupation. Percentages allowed us to indicate relative change over time and between women and men without resorting to often incomprehensible statistical measures.

But the experience of working with available quantitative data was extremely frustrating. The concepts and techniques used in data collection often excluded women's experience, even when the data were tabulated by sex. Household work was invisible. Moreover, these data could tell us nothing about the nature and conditions of work in either the public or the private sphere. Influenced by these frustrations and by feminist critiques of mainstream methodology, we tried to combine the use of qualitative and quantitative techniques, using statistical data to establish the broad outlines of the segregation, and long, partially structured interviews to examine the nature and conditions of women's work. With other feminists, we rejected the view that social science research is entirely objective, and that the researcher is uncommitted and omniscient, able to understand far better than those being studied what was really happening in their lives. "We are seeking information both on how the work was structured, and on women's approaches to their work and perceptions of it. Obviously the objective and subjective are intimately connected, indeed often inseparable" (Armstrong and Armstrong, 1983c:224). The interviewers were committed feminists with experience in feminist research, teaching, and organizations. Although we "arranged their responses to fit into an ordered framework, and abbreviated some for the sake of pertinence and clarity, we ... tried to let the women speak for themselves" (Armstrong and Armstrong, 1983c:iv). Our theory had developed along with the research and been altered by the research.

We explicitly rejected the temptation to gain traditional legitimacy by transforming our sixty-five interviews into numbers (although, interestingly, at least one feminist reviewer saw this as the major problem with the study). Instead we argued that

> the statistical representativity of the sample survey is lost, but what is gained is much more than a collection of anecdotes. The consistent patterns emerging from the 65 interviews used in this study suggest that we have found many of the common treads in women's work. The women who read this book will provide the real test of its validity. If it resonates well with their own experiences, if it both reflects their daily lives and sheds new light on them, then it will have fulfilled its most important requirement. We believe that the analysis of these interviews provides much more than a string of examples. It contributes to the task of exposing the nature and conditions of women's work. (Armstrong and Armstrong, 1983c:222)

This research served to increase our frustration with the available statistics and statistical techniques, but we were still convinced that some statistical analysis was essential in order to draw out long-term and national trends, and to set the stage for other, qualitative research. Although we agreed with Margaret Benston (1982:56) that "what is needed is a methodology that does not, in fact, relegate the non-quantifiable aspects of a problem to secondary status but instead attempts some kind of integration of this into scientific practice," we also felt that feminists had to transform the quantifiable data and their techniques of analysis. When we were asked, along with other researchers, to participate in a 1982 conference on data requirements to support research into women and the Canadian economy, we tried to put some of these concerns into writing, arguing that

> statistics are not all they are cracked up to be. The way data are collected and tabulated, the way questions are asked and not asked, the way government programmes and policies are structured and the way in which history is considered, all influence the data and in the process often leave out and sometimes misrepresent the position of women. Qualitative data, while not free of faults, can provide an effective complement to quantitative techniques, checking the results, suggesting alternative areas and methods for research and filling in the numbers with the actual experiences of women. (Armstrong and Armstrong, 1983a:37)

Because theory and method are intimately connected, an appropriate methodology involves more than simply adding women in. It involves a transformation of both quantitative and qualitative techniques. It involves examining different processes in different ways because the different work of women and men means that they experience the world in different ways. We were arguing the need for alternative techniques rather than outlining what these techniques would be. We would now argue, however, that they should involve methods that could get at dialectical processes, and that standard mathematical measures, however sophisticated, can only measure linear or partial relationships, not contradictory ones.

Of course, we were not alone in our critiques of traditional academic research methods, or in our search for alternative approaches. The ongoing Luxton, Seccombe, Livingston, and Corman study of Hamilton households combines large-scale survey techniques with intensive interviews. Jennifer Penney's (1983) study of women's work allowed women in the labour force to define the nature and conditions of their work. The papers brought together by Kinnear and Mason in *Women and Work* (1982) testified to the lacunae in existing data bases. Papers from conferences of the Canadian Research Institute for the Advancement of Women (CRIAW) published in *Knowledge Reconsidered: A Feminist Overview* (CRIAW:1984), and by Jill Vickers in *Taking Sex into Account* (1984) collectively demonstrated "the need for new and different questions, focusing on new themes, researched through new methods, and offering new answers" (Gow and Leo, 1984:x); the need to learn "how and when to take sex 'into account' as a variable" (Vickers, 1984:4). In *Feminism in Canada* (Miles and Finn, 1982), the articles by Vickers and by Benston argued for a committed feminist scholarship; those by Cohen, Wine, Pierson, and Prentice and Finn exposed problems for feminist scholarship within their disciplines, and Levine's established the importance of personal experience in social science research. In *On the Treatment of the Sexes in Research*, Eichler and Lapointe (1985) offered specific criteria for determining sexism in research and suggested means for developing a sex-conscious research strategy. Most recently, the twelve authors included in Thom's (1989) *The Effects of Feminist Approaches on Research Methodologies* have emphasized that "research originates from an individual's particular set of interests and is invariably tied to the historical location of that individual" and that "women's location in history is as important as that of men." (11) All these critiques have contributed to the development of a new feminist methodology.

There has been convergence on questions of methodology and subject. Although participants at the 1985 United Nations conference in Nairobi may still have disagreed about whether certain issues are political or are women's issues, and although some women objected to the scope of the party leaders' TV debate on women during the 1984 Canadian election campaign, few feminists in Canada would limit the range of issues to a narrowly prescribed, finite area. And most would agree that new qualitative methods are needed for investigation into women's work. More and more feminists are combining qualitative and quantitative techniques, and, in the process, are transforming these techniques. The old dichotomies between qualitative and quantitative research and between women's issues and people's issues appear less frequently.

Relating Theory and Empirical Research

Although some debates about methodology have disappeared, there are still frequent disagreements about the importance of theory and its relationship to empirical research. Two quite different approaches have been evident and both have come under attack.

An exclusive focus on theory was evident in much of the domestic labour debate. In her review of the articles brought together by Bonnie Fox (1980) in *Hidden in the Household*, Roberta Hamilton (1981:115) criticized the authors for concentrating on developing "a theory which can be appealed to for answers without having to engage in the untidy and painstaking process of encountering the social world." Cerise Morris (1987:121) went much further, criticizing all marxist-feminists for trying "'to fit women in' to a male-centered world view in which the personal gets lost in the realm of 'ideas' and 'structures'."

While some have focused on theory, others have rejected the use of theory, arguing instead for an exclusive concentration on women's experiences. Women were to speak for themselves, providing their own explanations for their work. This approach, too, has encountered its share of criticism. Briskin (1989:91) has argued that this

> tendency to anti-intellectualism and anti-theory in the women's movement which accompanies the emphasis on experience promotes individualism, on the one hand, and on the other, promotes the identification of women, not with reason, but with nature — both of which are ideologies of patriarchal capitalism.

Although Dawn Currie (1988:233) agreed that "feminist theory should not become 'expert's theory', rejecting other women's experiences," she disagreed "with the notion that structures and institutions are not oppressive forces and that they are constructed entirely out of everyday life."

Although both these tendencies can be found in the Canadian feminist literature, most feminists have combined the development of theory with empirical research. Most would agree that women should speak for themselves and not be squeezed into predetermined theoretical categories. But the relationship between theory and research is constantly being worked out in the process of conducting empirical research.

Dorothy Smith (1987:153) has argued for a "method beginning from where women are as subjects" rather than one that begins with theoretical constructs. "It is the individual's working knowledge of her everyday world that provides the beginning of the inquiry" (154). Her approach, which she calls "institutional ethnography," is intended to "explicate ... institutional relations determining everyday worlds and hence how the local organization of the latter may be explored to uncover their ordinary invisible determinations in relations that generalize and are generalized." (160) Theory has a place, but it grows out of knitting together these various "standpoints of women."

By contrast, we argued that it is necessary to begin with an explicit theoretical framework because theory is what guides us to select the area and people of concern (Armstrong and Armstrong, 1983a). Women never do simply speak for themselves in empirical research, because as researchers we have already chosen to record what some women say, prompted them to talk about particular aspects of their lives, and edited parts of their representations and interpretations. This does not mean that we should shape the people to fit the theory. Rather, we needed a clear theoretical framework that could be altered or transformed both by the research and by the women's descriptions and analyses of their daily lives.

More recently, Dawn Currie (1988:235, emphasis in original) has argued for "grounded theory." By this she meant an approach in which "*generating the explanation cannot be separated from the process of conducting research.*" The emphasis is on "*theory as process*: that is, theory as an ever-developing entity rather than a perfect product."

Most feminists would now agree that theory building is a continuous process that remains dynamic because it is challenged by research on women's and men's experiences in, actions on, and perceptions of the real world. Increasingly, feminists are "grounding" their research in the way Currie suggests. But "the untidy and painstaking process of encountering the social world" has seldom been absent from Canadian feminist theory.

Conclusion

There are still crucial debates within and between various perspectives on what should be studied and how it should be studied. Materialists continue to begin their analyses with an explicit theoretical framework, as well as a focus on work and how that work is structured by the search for profit. Many use quantitative means to examine structural constraints and qualitative techniques to provide details about historically specific and concrete situations. But what has been defined as work has been expanded to include women's particular part in reproduction, and the boundaries of what can be properly addressed only in sex-conscious fashion have expanded enormously. That the theoretical and methodological interests of materialists have expanded does not mean agreement on how to proceed; rather, it means greater scope for materialist debate.

Radical feminists, on the other hand, continue to focus on the origins of domination and on the "basis for unique feminist values and a feminist vision" (Miles, 1985:16), relying primarily on qualitative techniques for their evidence. What this unique vision entails and how the origins of domination can be related to its elimination are matters of debate among theorists working from this perspective. What is clear, at least to us, is that, "the justification of feminist scholarship must rest not on a special domain (women) or a special kind of empathy (sexual affinity) but on a set of principles of inquiry: a feminist philosophy of science" (McCormack, 1981:3).

Chapter Nine
Conclusion

It is, of course, impossible to do justice in one monograph to the wide-ranging and rich English Canadian literature theorizing women's work. The problem is compounded by two factors. First, there is the important influence exerted on English Canadian debates by British and American theory, and, to a lesser extent, by French Canadian and other theory, coupled with the involvement of English Canadians in theoretical developments worldwide, which make it difficult to restrict the discussion to English Canada. Second, there is the inevitable tendency for theories of women's work to extend to all aspects of women's subordination, which makes it difficult to restrict the discussion to theories about work. We have tried to use examples to outline the major themes in the current waves of feminist analysis of women's work, limiting the discussion to those English Canadians who have focused on women's work.

To some extent, English Canadian theorists have been characterized by their openness to criticism both from within their particular framework and from without. This openness which has perhaps arisen from the small size of the intellectual and political community, has contributed to the development not only of more sophisticated and complex theory, but also of a convergence in many areas. All agree that any adequate theory of women's work must consider domestic and wage labour, bodies and socially constructed possibilities, ideas and material conditions, resistance, and the state. All agree that research must be sex-conscious. Increasingly, theorists of various persuasions have become aware that technology is a central factor in all of these areas. But the question of how these issues are to be theorized and researched is still a central facet of the debates. Theory simplifies and provides the basis for both research and strategy. As changing economic and social conditions threaten a retreat not only from the welfare state but also from the gains made by women, theorization of women's work becomes an even more crucial concern.

REFERENCES

Acton, Janice, Penny Goldsmith, and Bonnie Shepard, eds. *Women at Work: Ontario, 1850-1930*. Toronto: Women's Educational Press, 1974.

Adamson, Nancy, Linda Briskin, and Margaret McPhail, *Feminist Organizing For Change: The Contemporary Women's Movement in Canada*. Toronto: Oxford University Press, 1988

Allingham, John D., *Women Who Work: Part 1. The Relative Importance of Age, Education and Marital Status for Participation in the Labour Force* (Statistics Canada Cat. 71-509.) Ottawa: Queen's Printer, 1967.

Allingham, John D. and Byron G. Spencer, *Women Who Work: Part 2. Married Women in the Labour Force: The Influence of Age, Education, and Child-Bearing Status and Residence* (Statistics Canada Cat. 71-514). Ottawa: Queen's Printer, 1968.

Ambert, Anne-Marie, *Sex Structure*. Second edition. Toronto: Longman Canada, 1976.

Ambert, Anne-Marie, *Divorce in Canada*. Don Mills: Academic Press, 1980.

Andersen, Margaret, ed. *Mother Was Not a Person*. Montreal: Black Rose, 1972.

Andrew, Caroline, "Women and the Welfare State," *Canadian Journal of Political Science*. XVIL (4, December 1984): 667-683.

Andrew, Caroline, *Getting the Word Out*. Ottawa: University of Ottawa Press, 1989.

Archibald, Kathleen, *Sex and the Public Service*. Ottawa: Queen's Printer, 1974.

Armstrong, Hugh and Pat Armstrong, "The Segregated Participation of Women in the Canadian Labour Force 1941-71," *The Canadian Review of Sociology and Anthropology*. 12 (4, Part 1, November 1975):370-384.

Armstrong, Pat, *Labour Pains: Women's Work in Crisis*. Toronto: The Women's Press, 1984.

Armstrong, Pat, "Comment on Eichler's 'And the Work Never Ends'," Paper presented at the Canadian Sociology and Anthropology Annual Meetings, Winnipeg, 1986.

Armstrong, Pat, "Where Have All the Nurses Gone?" *Healthsharing* 9 (3, June 1988):17-19.

Armstrong, Pat and Hugh Armstrong, *The Double Ghetto: Canadian Women and Their Segregated Work*. Toronto: McClelland and Stewart, 1978.

Armstrong, Pat and Hugh Armstrong, "A Framework For Policy Recommendations on Labour Force Work Flowing From *A Working Majority*," Paper presented to the Canadian Advisory Council on the Status of Women, 1982.

Armstrong, Pat and Hugh Armstrong, "Beyond Numbers: Problems with Quantitative Data," *Alternate Routes*. 1983a, 6:1-40.

Armstrong, Pat and Hugh Armstrong, "Beyond Sexless Class and Classless Sex: Towards Feminist Marxism," *Studies in Political Economy*. 10 (Winter 1983b):7-43.

Armstrong, Pat and Hugh Armstrong, *A Working Majority: What Women Must Do For Pay*. Ottawa: Supply and Services for the Canadian Advisory Council on the Status of Women, 1983c.

Armstrong, Pat and Hugh Armstrong, *The Double Ghetto: Canadian Women and Their Segregated Work*. Revised edition. Toronto: McClelland and Stewart, 1984a.

Armstrong, Pat and Hugh Armstrong, "More on Marxism and Feminism: A Response to Patricia Connelly," *Studies in Political Economy*. 15 (Fall 1984b):179-184.

Armstrong, Pat and Hugh Armstrong, "Political Economy and the Household: Rejecting Separate Spheres," *Studies in Political Economy*. 17 (Summer 1985):167-177.

Armstrong, Pat and Hugh Armstrong, "Taking Women Into Account: Redefining and Intensifying Employment in Canada," in Jane Jenson, Elizabeth Hagen, and Ceallaigh Reddy, eds. *Feminization of the Labour Force*. Cambridge: Polity Press, 1988.

Armstrong, Pat and Hugh Armstrong, "Lessons from Pay Equity," Paper presented to the Conference on Gender and Class, Antwerp, September, 1989.

Armstrong, Pat, Jacqueline Choiniere, Chris Gabriel, and Jon Kainer, "Female Dominated Sectors: Health Care," Report prepared for the Ontario Pay Equity Commission, 1988.

The Bank Book Collective, *An Account to Settle. The Story of the United Bank Workers* (SORWUC). Vancouver: Press Gang, 1979.

Barnsley, Jan, "Feminist Action, Institutional Reaction," *Resources for Feminist Research*. Special Issue. 17 (3, September 1988).

Baxter, Sheila, *No Way to Live: Poor Women Speak Out*. Vancouver: New Star Books, 1988.

Bayefsky, E., "Part-Time Work: Patterns of Implementation," in E.D. Pask, K.E. Mahoney and C.A. Brown, eds. *Women, The Law and the Economy*. Toronto: Butterworths, 1985.

Bell, Laurie, "Introduction," in Laurie Bell, ed. *Good Girls, Bad Girls: Sex Trade Workers and Feminists Face to Face*. Toronto: The Women's Press, 1987.

Bellew, M., "A Study Into Part-Time Work in the Maritimes," *Communique'*. (Winter 1982-83) The Institute for the Study of Women, Mount St. Vincent University.

Benston, Margaret, "The Political Economy of Women's Liberation," *Monthly Review*. xxi (4, September 1969):13-27.

Benston, Margaret, "Feminism and the Critique of Scientific Method," in Angela Miles and Geraldine Finn, eds. *Feminism in Canada*. Montreal: Black Rose, 1982.

Benston, Margaret, "For Women, The Chips are Down," in Jan Zimmerman, ed. *The Technological Woman: Interfacing with Tomorrow*. New York: Praeger, 1983.

Benston, Margaret, "Feminism and System Design: Questions of Control," in Winnie Tomm, ed. *The Effects of Feminist Approaches on Research Methodology*. Waterloo: Wilfred Laurier Press, 1989.

Bercovitch, Joan, "Civil Law Regulation of Reproductive Technologies," *Canadian Journal of Women and the Law*. 1 (2, 1986):385-406.

Bernard, Elaine, *The Long Distance Feeling: A History of the Telecommunications Workers' Union*. Vancouver: New Star Books, 1982.

Bernstein, Judy, Peggy Morton, Linda Seese, and Myrna Wood, "Sisters, Brothers, Lovers ... Listen" in *Women Unite!* Toronto: The Women's Press, (1967) 1972.

Boehnert, Joanna, "The Psychology of Women," in Sandra Burt, Lorraine Code, and Lindsay Dorney, eds. *Changing Patterns: Women in Canada.* Toronto: McClelland and Stewart, 1988.

Boulet, Jac-André and Laval Lavallée, *The Changing Economic Status of Women.* Ottawa: Supply and Services Canada, for the Economic Council of Canada, 1984.

Bouma, Gary and Wilma Bouma, *Fertility Control: Canada's Lively Social Problem.* Don Mills: Longman Canada, 1975.

Boyd, Monica, "English Canadian and French Canadian Attitudes Toward Women: Results of the Canadian Gallup Polls," *Journal of Comparative Family Studies* 6 (2, 1975a):153-169.

Boyd, Monica, "The Status of Immigrant Women in Canada," *Canadian Review of Sociology and Anthropology.* 12 (4, Part 1, 1975b):406-423.

Boyd, Monica, "The Double Negative: Female Immigrants in the Canadian Labour Force," Paper presented at the Annual Meeting of the Population Association of America. Denver, April 1980.

Boyd, Monica, *Canadian Attitudes Toward Women: Thirty Years of Change.* Ottawa: Supply and Services Canada, for the Women's Bureau, Labour Canada, 1984.

Bradbury, Bettina, "Pigs, Cows and Boarders: Non-wage Forms of Survival Among Montreal Families, 1861-91," *Labour/Le Travail.* 14, 1984:9-46.

Braverman, Harry, *Labor and Monopoly Capital: The Degradation of Work in the Twentieth Century.* New York: Monthly Review Press, 1974.

Briskin, Linda, "Socialist Feminism: From the Standpoint of Practice," *Studies in Political Economy.* 30 (Fall 1989).

Briskin, Linda and Lynda Yantz, eds. *Union Sisters: Women in the Labour Movement.* Toronto: The Women's Press, 1983.

Brodribb, Somer, "Off the Pedestal and onto the Block? Motherhood, Reproductive Technologies and the Canadian State," *Canadian Journal of Women and the Law.* 1 (2, 1986):407-423.

Burnett, Jean, ed. *Looking Into My Sisters' Eyes: An Exploration in Women's History.* Toronto: The Multicultural History Society of Ontario, 1986.

Burstyn, Varda, "Masculine Dominance and the State," in Ralph Miliband and John Saville, eds. *The Socialist Register 1983*. London: The Merlin Press, 1983.

Calvert, John, *Government Unlimited: The Corporate Takeover of the Public Sector in Canada*. Ottawa: The Canadian Centre for Policy Alternatives, 1984.

Cameron, Barbara, "Labour Market Discrimination and Affirmative Action," in Jill McCalla Vickers, ed. *Taking Sex into Account*. Ottawa: Carleton University Press, 1984.

Canada, Advisory Committee on Reconstruction, *Post-war Problems of Women: Final Report of the Subcommittee*. Ottawa: King's Printer, 1944.

Canada, Royal Commission on Equality in Employment, *Equality in Employment*. Ottawa: Supply and Services Canada, 1984.

Canada, Royal Commission on the Status of Women, *Report*. Ottawa: Information Canada, 1970.

Canadian Advisory Council on the Status of Women, *Part-Time Work: Part-Time Rights*. A Brief Presented to the Commission of Enquiry into Part-Time Work. Ottawa: Author, 1982.

Canadian Advisory Council on the Status of Women, *The Status of Women and the CBC*. A Brief by the Canadian Advisory Council on the Status of Women to the Canadian Radio-Television and Telecommunications Commission. Ottawa, 1978.

Canadian National Railway Co. and Canadian Human Rights Commission, Federal Court of Appeal, 147 D.L.R. 3rd 312 F.C.A., 1983.

Canadian Research Institute for the Advancement of Women/Institut canadien de recherches pour l'avancement de la femme, *Knowledge Reconsidered: A Feminist Overview*. Ottawa: CRIAW/ICRAF, 1984.

Caplan, Paula, *The Myth of Women's Masochism*. New York: E.P. Dutton, 1985.

Caplan, Paula and Ian Hall-McCorquodale, "Mother-Blaming in Major Clinical Journals," *American Journal of Orthopsychiatry*. 55 (3, 1985):345-353.

Carty, Linda and Dionne Brand, "'Visible Minority' Women — A Creation of the Canadian State," *Resources For Feminist Research*. 17 (3, 1988):39-42.

Clark, Susan and Andrew Harvey, "The Sexual Division of Labour: The Use of Time," *Atlantis*. 2 (1, Fall 1976):46-55.

Code, Lorraine, "Feminist Theory," in Sandra Burt, Lorraine Code, and Lindsay Dorney, eds. *Changing Patterns: Women in Canada*. Toronto: McClelland and Stewart, 1988.

Coffey, Mary Anne, "Of Father Born: A Lesbian Feminist Critique of the Ontario Law Reform Commission Recommendations on Artificial Insemination," *Canadian Journal of Women and the Law*. 1 (2, 1986):407-423.

Cohen, Marjorie Griffin, "The Problem of Studying 'Economic Man'," in Angela Miles and Geraldine Fenn, eds. *Feminism in Canada*. Montreal: Black Rose, 1982.

Cohen, Marjorie Griffin, *Free Trade and the Future of Women's Work*. Toronto: Garamond Press and the Canadian Centre for Policy Alternatives, 1987.

Cohen, Marjorie Griffin, *Women's Work, Markets, and Economic Development in Nineteenth-Century Ontario*. Toronto: University of Toronto Press, 1988.

Collins, Kevin, *Women and Pensions*. Ottawa: The Canadian Council on Social Development, 1978.

Connelly, M. Patricia, *Last Hired: First Fired*. Toronto: The Women's Press, 1978.

Connelly, M. Patricia, "Women's Work and the Family Wage in Canada," in Anne Hoiberg, ed. *Women and the World of Work*. New York: Plenum, 1982.

Connelly, M. Patricia, "On Marxism and Feminism," *Studies in Political Economy*. 12 (Fall 1983):153-161.

Connelly, M. Patricia and Pat Armstrong, "Feminist Political Economy," *Studies in Political Economy*. 30 (Fall 1989).

Connelly, M. Patricia and Martha MacDonald, "Women's Work: Domestic and Wage Labour in a Nova Scotia Community," *Studies in Political Economy*. 10 (Winter 1983):45-72.

Cook, Gail, ed. *Opportunity for Choice*. Ottawa:Information Canada, 1976.

Cornish, Mary and Laurel Ritchie, *Getting Organized: Building a Union*. Toronto: The Women's Press, 1980.

Cowan, Ruth Swartz, *More Work For Mother: The Ironies of Household Technology from the Open Hearth to the Microwave*. New York: Basic Books, 1983.

Currie, Dawn, "Re-Thinking What We Do and How We Do It: A Study of Reproductive Decisions," *Canadian Review of Sociology and Anthropology*. 25 (2, May 1988):231-253.

Denton, Margaret and Alfred Hunter, *Equality in the Workplace. Economic Sectors and Gender Discrimination in Canada: A Critique and Test of Block and Walker ... and Some New Evidence*. Ottawa: Supply and Services Canada, for the Women's Bureau, Labour Canada, 1984.

Dixon, Marlene, "Ideology, Class and Liberation," in Margaret Andersen, ed. *Mother Was Not a Person*. Montreal: Black Rose Books, 1972.

Doyle, Cassie and Janet McClain, "Women, The Forgotten Housing Consumers," in Jill McCalla Vickers, ed. *Taking Sex Into Account*. Ottawa: Carleton University Press, 1984.

Duffy, Ann, Nancy Mandell and Norene Pupo, *Few Choices: Women, Work and Family*. Toronto: Garamond Press, 1989.

Dulude, Louise, *Women and Aging: A Report on the Rest of Our Lives*. Ottawa: The Canadian Advisory Council on the Status of Women, 1978.

Dulude, Louise, *Love, Marriage and Money. An Analysis of Financial Relations Between the Spouses*. Ottawa: The Canadian Advisory Council of the Status of Women, 1984.

Eichler, Margrit, "Women As Personal Dependents," in Marylee Stephenson, ed. *Women in Canada*. Toronto: New Press, 1973.

Eichler, Margrit, "Sociological Research on Women in Canada," *Canadian Review of Sociology and Anthropology*. 12 (4, November 1975):474-481.

Eichler, Margrit, "The Prestige of the Occupation Housewife," in Patricia Marchak, ed. *The Working Sexes*. Vancouver: Institute of Industrial Relations, University of British Columbia, 1977.

Eichler, Margrit, "Women's Unpaid Labour," *Atlantis*. 3 (2, Spring 1978):52-62.

Eichler, Margrit, *The Double Standard: A Feminist Critique of Feminist Social Science*. London: Croon Helm, 1980.

Eichler, Margrit, *Families in Canada Today: Recent Changes and Their Policy Consequences*. Toronto: Gage, 1983.

Eichler, Margrit, "And the Work Never Ends: Feminist Contributions," *The Canadian Review of Sociology and Anthropology*. 22 (5, February 1985):619-644.

Eichler, Margrit, "The Relationship Between Sexist, Non-Sexist, Woman-Centred and Feminist Research in the Social Sciences," in Geta Hofmann Nemiroff, ed. *Women and Men*. Toronto: Fitzhenry and Whiteside, 1987.

Eichler, Margrit and Jeanne Lapointe, *On the Treatment of the Sexes in Research*. Ottawa: Supply and Services Canada, for the Social Sciences and Humanities Research Council of Canada, 1985.

Estable, Alma, "Immigrant Women in Canada — Current Issues," Background paper prepared for the Canadian Advisory Council on the Status of Women, 1986.

Evans, Patricia M. and Eilene L. McIntyre, "Welfare, Work Incentives, and the Single Mother: An Interprovincial Comparison," in Jacqueline S. Ismael, ed. *The Canadian State: Evolution and Transition*. Alberta: The University of Alberta Press, 1987.

Findlay, Sue, "Representation and Regulation: The Role of State Bureaucracy in Limiting Equal Employment Opportunities for Women," *Canada Woman's Studies*. 6 (4, Winter 1985):30-34.

Findlay, Sue, "Facing the State: The Politics of the Women's Movement Reconsidered," in Heather Jon Maroney and Meg Luxton, eds. *Feminism and Political Economy*. Toronto: Methuen, 1987.

Findlay, Sue, "Feminist Struggles With the Canadian State: 1966-1988," *Resources in Feminist Research*. 17 (3, September 1988):5-9.

Finn, Geraldine, "On the Oppression of Women in Philosophy," in Angela Miles and Geraldine Finn, eds. *Feminism in Canada*. Montreal: Black Rose, 1982.

Firestone, Shulamith, *The Dialectic of Sex*. New York: Bantam, 1970.

Fitzgerald, Maureen, Connie Guberman, and Margie Wolfe, eds. *Still Ain't Satisfied! Canadian Feminism Today*. Toronto: The Women's Press, 1982.

Fox, Bonnie, "Women's Double Work Day: Twentieth Century Changes in the Reproduction of Daily Life," in Bonnie Fox, ed. *Hidden in the Household: Women's Domestic Labour Under Captialism*. Toronto: The Women's Press, 1980.

Fox, Bonnie, ed. *Hidden in the Household: Women's Domestic Labour Under Capitalism*. Toronto: The Women's Press, 1980.

Fox, Bonnie, "The Female Reserve Army of Labour: The Argument and Some Pertinent Findings," *Atlantis*. 7 (Fall 1981):45-56.

Fox, Bonnie, "Conceptualizing Patriarchy," *The Canadian Review of Sociology and Anthropology*. 25, (2, May 1988):163-182.

Fox, Bonnie, *A Feminist Critique of Recent Work on Status Attainment and Social Class*. Research Paper No. 204, Department of Sociology, University of Toronto, March, 1989.

Fox, Bonnie and John Fox, "Women in the Labour Market 1931-1981: Exclusion and Competition," *The Canadian Review of Sociology and Anthropology*. 23 (1986):1-22.

Frager, Ruth, "Class Politics, Ethnic Identity and the Barriers to Feminist Consciousness," *Studies in Political Economy*. 30 (Fall 1989).

Franklin, Ursula Martius, "Will Women Change Technology or Will Technology Change Women?" in Canadian Research Institute for the Advancement of Women/Institut canadien de recherches pour l'avancement de la femme, ed. *Knowledge Reconsidered: A Feminist Overview*. Ottawa: CRIAW/ICRAF, 1984.

Gannagé, Charlene, *Double Day, Double Bind: Women Garment Workers*. Toronto, The Women's Press, 1986.

Gaskell, Jane, "Education and Job Opportunities For Women: Patterns of Enrolment and Economic Returns," in Naomi Hersom and Dorothy E. Smith, eds. *Women and the Canadian Labour Force*. Ottawa: The Social Sciences and Humanities Research Council of Canada, 1982.

Gaskell, Jane, "Conceptions of Skill and the Work of Women: Some Historical and Political Issues," in Roberta Hamilton and Michèle Barrett, eds. *The Politics of Diversity*. Montreal: Book Centre, 1986.

Gow, June and Willadean Leo, "Preface," in CRIAW/ICRAFed. *Knowledge Reconsidered: A Feminist Overview*. Ottawa: CRIAW/ICRAF, 1984.

Goyder, John, "Income Differences Between the Sexes: Findings from a National Survey," *The Canadian Review of Sociology and Anthropology*. 18 (1981):321-342.

Greenglass, Esther, "The Psychology of Women; Or, the High Cost of Achievement," in Marylee Stephenson, ed. *Women in Canada*. Toronto: New Press, 1973.

Greenglass, Esther, *A World of Difference: Gender Roles in Perspective*. Toronto: John Wiley and Sons, 1982.

Guberman, Connie and Margie Wolfe, eds. *No Safe Place: Violence Against Women and Children*. Toronto: The Women's Press, 1985.

Guettel, Charnie, *Marxism and Feminism*. Toronto: The Women's Press, 1974.

Gunderson, Morley, "Work Patterns," in Gail A. Cook, ed. *Opportunity for Choice*. Ottawa: Statistics Canada, in cooperation with C.D. Howe Research Institute, 1976.

Gunderson, Morley, "Discrimination, Equal Pay, and Equal Opportunities," in W. Craig Riddell (research coordinator). *Work and Pay: The Canadian Labour Market*. Toronto: University of Toronto Press, in cooperation with the Royal Commission on the Economic Union and Development Prospects for Canada and the Canadian Government Publishing Centre, 1985.

Haas, Jack and William Shaffir, *Shaping Identity in Canadian Society*. Scarborough: Prentice-Hall Canada, 1978.

Hamilton, Roberta, *The Liberation of Women*. London: George Allen and Unwin, 1978.

Hamilton, Roberta, "Working At Home," *Atlantis*. 7 (1, Fall 1981):114-126.

Hamilton, Roberta, "The Collusion with Patriarchy: a Psychoanalytic Account," *Alterate Routes*. 6 (1983):41-60.

Hamilton, Roberta and Michèle Barrett, eds. "The Politics of Diversity. Montreal: Book Centre, 1986.

Hayden, Dolores, *The Grand Domestic Revolution: A History of Feminist Designs for American Homes, Neighborhoods, and Cities.* Cambridge, Mass.: MIT Press, 1981.

Heitlinger, Alena, *Reproduction, Medicine and The Socialist State.* London: Macmillan, 1987.

Henshel, Anne-Marie, *Sex Structure.* Don Mills: Longman Canada, 1973.

Horowitz, Gad, *Basic and Surplus Repression in Psychoanalytic Theory: Freud, Reich and Marcuse.* Toronto: University of Toronto Press, 1977.

Horowitz, Gale and Michael Kaufman, ''Male Sexuality: Toward a Theory of Liberation,'' in Michael Kaufman, ed. *Beyond Patriarchy.* Toronto: Oxford University Press, 1987.

Jenson, Jane, ''Gender and Reproduction, or Babies and the State,'' *Studies in Political Economy.* 20 (1986).

Johnson, Laura C. and Janice Dineen, *The Kin Trade: The Day Care Crisis in Canada.* Toronto: McGraw-Hill Ryerson, 1981.

Johnson, Laura C. with Robert E. Johnson, *The Seam Allowance.* Toronto: The Women's Press, 1982.

Johnson, Leo, ''The Political Economy of Ontario Women in the Nineteenth Century,'' in Janice Action, Penny Goldsmith and Bonnie Shepard, eds. *Women at Work: Ontario, 1850-1930.* Toronto: The Women's Press, 1974.

Kealey, Linda, ed. *A Not Unreasonable Claim: Women and Reform in Canada, 1880s-1920s.* Toronto: The Women's Press, 1979.

Keynes, John Maynard, *The General Theory of Employment, Interest and Money.* New York: Harcourt, Brace, 1936.

Kinnear, Mary and Greg Mason, eds. *Women and Work.* Winnipeg: The Institute for Social and Economic Research, University of Manitoba, 1982.

Klein, Alice and Wayne Roberts, ''Beseiged Innocence: The 'Problem' and Problems of Working Women — Toronto, 1896-1914,'' in Janice Acton, Penny Goldsmith and Bonnie Shepard, eds. *Women at Work: Ontario, 1850-1930.* Toronto: The Women's Press, 1974.

Kreps, Bonnie, ''Radical Feminism 1,'' in *Women Unite!* Toronto: The Women's Press, 1972.

Labour Canada, *In the Chips: Opportunities, People, Partnerships.* Report of the Labour Canada Task Force on Micro-Electronics and Employment. Ottawa: Supply and Services Canada, 1982.

Labour Canada, *When I Grow Up ... Career Expectations and Aspirations of Canadian School Children.* Ottawa: Labour Canada, 1986.

Levine, Helen, "The Personal is Political: Feminism and the Helping Professions," in Angela Miles and Geraldine Finn, eds. *Feminism in Canada*. Montreal: Black Rose Books, 1982.

Levine, Helen and Alma Estable, *The Power Politics of Motherhood: A Feminist Critique of Theory and Practice*. Ottawa: Carleton University Press Mimeo, 1981.

Lewis, Debra, *Just Give Us The Money: A Discussion of Wage Discrimination and Pay Equity*. Vancouver: Women's Research Centre, 1988.
Likely, Jane, "Women and the Revolution," in *Women Unite!* Toronto: The Women's Press, 1972.

Lippman, Abby, "Access to Prenatal Screening Services: Who Decides?" *The Canadian Journal of Women and the Law*. 1 (2, 1986):434-445.

Lipsig-Mummé, Carla, "Organizing Women in the Clothing Trades: Homework and the 1983 Garment Strike in Canada," *Studies in Political Economy*. 22 (Spring 1987):41-72.

Livingstone, David and Meg Luxton, "Gender Consciousness at Work: Modification of the Male Breadwinner Norm Among Steelworkers and Their Spouses," *The Canadian Joural of Sociology and Anthropology*. 26 (2, May 1989):240-275.

Lowe, Graham S., *Women in the Administrative Revolution*. Toronto: University of Toronto Press, 1987.

Lowe, Graham S. and Harvey Krahn, "Where Wives Work: The Relative Effects of Situational and Attitudinal Factors," *The Canadian Journal of Sociology* 10 (1, Winter 1985):1-22.

Lowe, Graham S. and Herbert Northcott, *Under Pressure: A Study of Job Stress*. Toronto: Garamond Press, 1986.

Luxton, Meg, *More Than a Labour of Love: Three Generation of Women's Work in the Home*. Toronto: The Women's Press, 1980.

Luxton, Meg, "Taking on the Double Day: Housewives as a Reserve Army of Labour," *Atlantis*. 2 (1, Fall 1981):12-22.

Luxton, Meg, "The Home: A Contested Terrain," in Maureen Fitzgerald, Connie Guberman, and Margie Wolfe, eds. *Still Ain't Satisfied*. Toronto: The Women's Press, 1982.

Luxton, Meg, "Two Hands for the Clock: Changing Patterns in the Gendered Division of Labour in the Home," *Studies in Political Economy*. 12 (Fall 1983):27-44

Luxton, Meg, "Conceptualizing Women in Anthropology and Sociology," in CRIAW/ICRAF, ed. *Knowledge Reconsidered: A Feminist Overview*. Ottawa: CRIAW/ICRAF, 1984.

MacDonald, Martha, "Implications For Understanding Women in the Labour Force of Labour Market Segmentation Analysis," in Naomi Hersom and Dorothy R. Smith, eds. *Women in the Canadian Labour Force.* Ottawa: Supply and Services Canada, 1982.

MacDonald, Martha, "Economics and Feminism: The Dismal Science," *Studies in Political Economy.* 15 (Winter 1984):151-178.

MacDonald, Martha and Patricia M. Connelly, "Class and Gender in Nova Scotia Fishing Communities," *Studies in Political Economy.* 30 (Fall 1989).

Mackie, Marlene, "Gender Socialization in Childhood and Adolescence," in K. Ishwaran, ed. *Childhood and Adolescence in Canada.* Toronto: McGraw-Hill Ryerson, 1979.

Mackie, Marlene, *Exploring Gender Relations: A Canadian Perspective.* Toronto: Butterworths, 1983.

Mackie, Marlene, *Constructing Women and Men: Gender Socialization.* Toronto: Holt, Rinehart and Winston, 1987.

MacLeod, Catherine, "Women in Production: The Toronto Dressmakers' Strike of 1931," in Janice Acton, Penny Goldsmith, and Bonnie Shepard, eds. *Women at Work: Ontario, 1850-1930.* Toronto: The Women's Press, 1974.

MacLeod, Linda, *Wife Battering in Canada: The Vicious Circle.* Ottawa: Supply and Services Canada, for the Canadian Advisory Council on the Status of Women, 1980.

Mahon, Rianne, "Canadian Public Policy: The Unequal Structure of Representation," in Leo Panitch, ed. *The Canadian State: Political Economy and Political Power.* Toronto: University of Toronto Press, 1977.

Mandell, Nancy, "Roles and Interactions," in Lorne Tepperman and R. Sack Richardson, eds. *The Social World.* Toronto: McGraw-Hill Ryerson, 1986.

Marchak, Patricia M., "The Canadian Labour Farce: Jobs for Women," in Marylee Stephenson, ed. *Women in Canada.* Toronto: New Press, 1973.

Maroney, Heather Jon, "Embracing Motherhood: New Feminist Theory," *The Canadian Journal of Political and Social Theory.* IX (1-2, Winter/Spring 1985):40-64.

Marsden, Lorna, "Some Problems with Research on Women in The Canadian Labour Force," *Atlantis.* 11 (2, Spring 1977):116-124.

Marsden, Lorna, "Livelihood: A Feminist View of the Sociology of Work," *Atlantis.* 3 (2, Spring 1978):5-20.

Marsden, Lorna, "'The Labour Force' is an Ideological Structure: A Guiding Note to the Labour Economists," *Atlantis.* 7 (2, Fall 1981):57-64.

Marshall, Barbara, "Feminist Theory and Critical Theory," *The Canadian Review of Sociology and Anthropology.* 25 (2, May 1988):208-230.

McClain, Janet with Cassie Doyle, *Women as Housing Consumers.* Ottawa: Mimeo, 1983.

McCormack, Thelma, "Toward a Non-Sexist Perspective on Social and Political Change," in M. Millmanard and R. Kanter, eds. *Another Voice.* New York: Anchor, 1975.

McCormack, Thelma, "The Professional Ethic and the Spirit of Capitalism," *Atlantis.* 5 (1, Fall 1979):132-141.

McCormack, Thelma, "Good Theory or Just Theory? Toward a Feminist Philosophy of Social Science," *Women's Studies International Quarterly.* 4 (1, 1981):1-12.

McCormack, Thelma, "Feminism and the New Crisis in Methodology," in Winnie Tomm, ed. *The Effects of Feminist Approaches on Research Methodologies.* Waterloo: Wilfred Laurier Press, 1989.

McDonnell, Kathleen, ed. *Adverse Effects.* Toronto: The Women's Press, 1986.

McLaren, Angus, "Birth Control and Abortion in Canada, 1870-1920," *Canadian Historical Review.* 59 (3, September 1978): 319-40.

McLaren, Angus, *Reproductive Rights.* London: Methuen, 1984.

McLaren, Angus and Arlene Tiger McLaren, *The Bedroom and The State: The Changing Practices and Policies of Contraception and Abortion in Canada, 1880-1980.* Toronto: McClelland and Stewart, 1986.

Meissner, Martin, Elizabeth W. Humphreys, Scott M. Meis, and William J. Scheu, "No Exit for Wives: Sexual Division of Labour and the Culmination of Household Demands," *The Canadian Review of Sociology and Anthropology* 12 (4, Part 1, November 1975):424-39.

Menzies, Heather, *Women and the Chip: Case Studies of the Effects of Informatics on Employment in Canada.* Montreal: The Institute of Research on Public Policy, 1981.

Menzies, Heather, *Computers on the Job.* Toronto: Lorimer, 1982.

Menzies, Heather, "The Future is Now," in Jacqueline Pelletier, ed. *The Future is Now: Women and the Impact of Technology.* Ottawa: Women and Technology Committee, 1983.

Messing, Karen, "Do Men and Women Have Different Jobs because of Their Biological Differences?" in Greta Hofman Nemiroff, ed. *Women and Men.* Toronto: Fitzhenry and Whiteside, 1986.

Messing, Karen and Jean-Pierre Reveret, "Are Women in Female Jobs For Their Health? A Study of Working Conditions and Health Effects in the Fish Processing Industry in Quebec," *International Journal of Health Services*. 13 (4, 1983):635-647.

Miles, Angela, "Ideological Hegemony in Political Discourse: Women's Specificity and Equality," in Angela Miles and Geraldine Finn, eds. *Feminism in Canada*. Montreal: Black Rose Books, 1982.

Miles, Angela, "Economism and Feminism," *Studies in Political Economy*. 11 (Summer 1983):197-209.

Miles, Angela, "Feminist Radicalism in the 1980s," *Canadian Journal of Political and Social Theory*. IX (1-2, 1985):16-39.

Miles, Angela and Geraldine Finn, eds. *Feminism in Canada*. Montreal: Black Rose Books, 1982.

Mitchell, Lorraine, "What Happened on the Way to the Bank: Some Questions About Pay Equity?" *Resources for Feminist Research*. 17 (3, 1988):64-66.

Morris, Cerise, "Against Determinism: The Case For Women's Liberation," in Greta Hofman Nemiroff, ed. *Women and Men*. Toronto: Fitzhenry and Whiteside, 1987.

Morton, Peggy, "Women's Work is Never Done," in *Women Unite!* Toronto: The Women's Press, 1972.

Moscovitch, Allan, *The Welfare State in Canada: A Selected Bibliography, 1840 to 1978*. Waterloo: Wilfrid Laurier University Press, 1983.

Myles, John, "The Expanding Middle: Some Canadian Evidence on the Deskilling Debate," *The Canadian Review of Sociology and Anthropology*. 25 (33, August 1988):335-364.

Nakamura, Alice, Masao Nakamura, and Dallas Cullen, in collaboration with Dwight Grand and Harriet Orcutt, *Employment and Earnings of Married Women*. (Cat. 99-760E). Ottawa: Supply and Services Canada, 1979.

Nakamura, Alice and Masao Nakamura, "A Survey of Research on the Work Behaviour of Canadian Women," in W. Craig Riddell (research coordinator) *Work and Pay: The Canadian Labour Market*. Toronto: University of Toronto Press, in cooperation with the Royal Commission on the Economic Union and Development Prospects for Canada and the Canadian Government Publishing Centre.

Ng, Roxanna, "The Social Construction of Immigrant Women in Canada," in Roberta Hamilton and Michèle Barrett, eds. *The Politics of Diversity*. Montreal: Book Center, 1986.

O'Brien, Mary, "The Dialectics of Reproduction," in J. King-Farlow and W. Shea, eds. *Contemporary Issues in Political Philosophy*. New York: Watson, 1976.

O'Brien, Mary, "Reproducing Marxist Man," in Lorainne Clark and Lynda Lange, eds. *The Sexism of Social and Political Theory*. Toronto: University of Toronto Press, 1979.

O'Brien, Mary, *The Politics of Reproduction*. London: Routeledge & Kegan Paul, 1981.

O'Brien, Mary, "Feminism and Revolution: Feminist Theory and Feminist Praxis," in Angela Miles and Geraldine Finn, eds. *Feminism in Canada*. Montreal: Black Rose Books, 1982.

O'Brien, Mary, "Reproductive Labour and The Creation of Value," *Atlantis*. 8 (Spring 1983):1-10.

O'Brien, Mary, "Hegemony and Superstructure: A Feminist Critique of Neo-Marxism," in Jill McCalla Vickers, ed. *Taking Sex Into Account*. Ottawa: Carleton University Press, 1984.

O'Brien, Mary, "Loving Wisdom," *Resources for Feminist Research*. 16 (3, September 1987):6-7.

Ornstein, Michael, *Equality in The Workplace: Accounting for Gender Differentials in Job Income in Canada: Results from a 1981 Survey*. Series A. No. 2. Ottawa: Women's Bureau, 1983.

Ostry, Sylvia, *The Female Worker in Canada*. (Statistics Canada Cat. 99-553). Ottawa: Queen's Printer, 1968.

Overall, Christine, "Reproductive Ethics: Feminist and Non-Feminist Approaches," *Canadian Journal of Women and the Law*. 1 (2, 1986):271-278.

Overall, Christine, "Sexuality, Parenting and Reproductive Choices," *Resources for Feminist Research*. 16 (3, September 1987):42-45.

Overall, Christine, *The Future of Human Reproduction*. Toronto: The Women's Press, 1989.

Panitch, Leo, ed. *The Canadian State: Political Economy and Political Power*. Toronto: University of Toronto Press, 1977.

Parent, Madeline, "Interview," *Studies in Political Economy*. 30 (Autumn 1989):13-36.

Parr, Joy, "Rethinking Work and Kinship in a Canadian Hosiery Town, 1910-1950," *Feminist Studies*. 13 (1, 1987a):137-162.

Parr, Joy, "The Skilled Emigrant and Her Kin: Gender, Culture, and Labour Recruitment," *Canadian Historical Review*. LXVIII (4, 1987b):530-551.

Peitchinis, Stephen, *Women At Work: Discrimination and Response*. Toronto: McClelland and Stewart, 1989.

Penney, Jennifer, *Hard Earned Wages: Women Fighting For Better Work*. Toronto: The Women's Press, 1983.

Phillips, Paul and Erin Phillips, *Women and Work*. Toronto: Lorimer, 1983.

Pierson, Ruth, "Women's Emancipation and the Recruitment of Women into the Labour Force in World War II," in Susan Mann Trofimenkoff and Alison Prentice, eds. *A Neglected Majority*. Toronto: McClelland and Stewart, 1977.

Pierson, Ruth Roach, *"They're Still Women After All.": the Second World War and Canadian Womanhood*. Toronto: McClelland and Stewart, 1986.

Pierson, Ruth and Alison Prentice, "Feminism and the Writing and Teaching of History," in Angela Miles and Geraldine Finn, eds. *Feminism in Canada*. Montreal: Black Rose Books, 1982.

Pike, Robert M. and Elia Zureik, eds. *Socialization and Values in Canadian Society. Volume II*. Toronto: McClelland and Stewart, 1975.

Prentice, Alison, "Writing Women into History: The History of Women's Work in Canada," *Atlantis*. 3 (2, Spring 1978):72-84.

Prentice, Alison, "The Feminization of Teaching," in Susan Mann Trofimenkoff and Alison Prentice, eds. *A Neglected Majority*. Toronto: McClelland and Stewart, 1977.

Prentice, Susan, "The 'Mainstreaming' of Day Care," *Resources For Feminist Research*. 17 (3, 1988):59-63.

Pryor, Edward T., "Canadian Husband-Wife Families: Labour Force Participation and Income Trends, 1971-1981," *The Labour Force*. (May 1984):93-109.

Pyke, S.W. and J.C. Stewart, "This Column is About Women: Women and Television," *The Ontario Psychologist*. 6 (1974):66-69.

Ramkhalawansignh, Ceta, "Women During the Great War," in Janice Acton, Penny Goldsmith, and Bonnie Shepard, eds. *Women at Work: Ontario, 1850-1930*. Toronto: The Women's Press, 1974.

Randall, Melanie, "Feminism and the State: Questions for Theory and Practice," *Resources for Feminist Research*. 17 (3, September 1988):10-16.

Rands, Jean, "Toward an Organization of Working Women," in *Women Unite!* Toronto: The Women's Press, 1972.

Rehner, Jan, *Infertility*. Toronto: Second Story Press, 1989.

Robinson, B.W. and E.D. Salamon, "Gender Role Socialization: A Review of the Literature," in E.D. Salamon and B.W. Robinson, eds. *Gender Roles: Doing What Comes Naturally?* Toronto: Methuen, 1987.

Rodgers, Sandra, "Fetal Rights and Maternal Rights: Is There a Conflict?" *Canadian Journal of Women and the Law*. 1 (2, 1986):456-469.

Romaniuc, A. *Fertility in Canada: From Baby-Boom to Baby-Bust*. Ottawa: Supply and Services Canada, for Statistics Canada, 1984.

Rossiter, Amy, *From Private to Public: A Feminist Exploration of Early Mothering*. Toronto: The Women's Press, 1988.

Russell, Susan, "Sex Role Socialization in High School: A Study in the Perpetuation of Patriarchal Culture." Ph.D. dissertation, University of Toronto, 1978.

Russell, Susan, "The Hidden Curriculum of School: Reproducing Gender and Class Hierarchies," in Roberta Hamilton and Michèle Barrett, eds. *The Politics of Diversity*. Montreal: Book Centre, 1986.

Seccombe, Wally, "The Housewife and Her Labour Under Capitalism," *New Left Review*. 83 (January-February, 1974):3-24.

Seccombe, Wally, "Domestic Labour and the Working-Class Household," in Bonnie Fox, ed. *Hidden in The Household: Women's Domestic Labour Under Capitalism*. Toronto: The Women's Press, 1980.

Seccombe, Wally, "Marxism and Demography: Household Forms and Fertility Regimes in Western European Transition," in James Dickinson and Bob Russell, eds. *Family, Economy and State: The Social Reproduction Process Under Capitalism*. Toronto: Garamond Press, 1986a.

Seccombe, Wally, "Reflections on the Domestic Labour Debate and Prospects for Marxist-feminist Synthesis," in Roberta Hamilton and Michèle Barrett, eds. *The Politics of Diversity*. Montreal: Book Center, 1986b.

Seward, Shirley and Kathryn McDade, "Immigrant Women in Canada —A Policy Perspective." Background paper prepared for the Canadian Advisory Council on the Status of Women, 1988.

Shack, Sybil, *The Two-Thirds Minority*. Toronto: The Governing Council of the University of Toronto, 1973.

Shaver, Fran, "The Feminist Defense of the Decriminalization of Prostitution," *Resources for Feminist Research*. 14 (4, December/January 1985-1986):38-39.

Skoulas, Nicholas, *Determinants of the Participation Rate of Married Women in the Canadian Labour Force: An Econometric Analysis*. (Statistics Canada, Cat. 71-522) Ottawa: Information Canada, 1974.

Smith, Dorothy E., "Women, the Family and Corporate Capitalism," in Marylee Stephenson, ed. *Women in Canada*. Toronto: New Press, 1973.

Smith, Dorothy E., "Women's Perspective as a Radical Critique of Sociology," *Sociological Inquiry*. 44 (1974):7-13.

Smith, Dorothy E., "An Analysis of Ideological Structures and How Women Are Excluded: Considerations For Academic Women," *The Canadian Review of Sociology and Anthropology*. 12 (4, 1975):353-369.

Smith, Dorothy E., *Feminism and Marxism*. Vancouver: New Star Books, 1977.

Smith, Dorothy E., "Institutional Ethnography: A Feminist Method," *Resources For Feminist Research*. 15 (1, March 1986).

Smith, Dorothy E., *The Everyday World as Problematic: A Feminist Sociology*. Toronto: University of Toronto Press, 1987.

Spinks, Sarah, "Sugar 'N' Spice ... the Socialization of Girl Children," in *Women Unite!* Toronto: The Women's Press, 1972.

Spencer, Byron G. and Dennis C. Featherstone, *Married Female Labour Force Participation: A Micro Study*. (Statistics Canada Cat. 71-516). Ottawa: Queen's Printer, 1970.

Statistics Canada, *Women in Canada*. A Statistical Report. (Cat. No. 89-503E) Ottawa: Supply and Services Canada, Queen's Printer, 1985.

Stephenson, Marylee, ed. *Women in Canada*. Toronto: New Press, 1973.

Storrie, Kathleen, ed. *Women: Isolation and Bonding: The Ecology of Gender*. Toronto: Methuen, 1987.

Strasser, Susan, *Never Done: A History of American Housework*. New York: Pantheon Books, 1982.

Sydie, R.A., *Natural Women, Cultured Men: A feminist Perspective on Sociological Theory*. Toronto: Methuen, 1987.

Tait, Janice, "Reproductive Technologies and the Rights of Disabled People," *Canadian Journal of Women and the Law* 1 (2, 1986)

Tomm, Winnie, ed. *The Effects of Feminist Approaches on Research Methodologies*. Waterloo: Wilfred Laurier Press, 1989.

Ursel, Jane, "The State and the Maintenance of Patriarchy: A Case Study of Family, Labour and Welfare Legislation in Canada," in James Dickinson and Bob Russell, eds. *Family, Economy and State: The Social Reproduction Process Under Capitalism*. Toronto: Garamond Press, 1986.

Valverde, Mariana, *Sex, Power and Pleasure*. Toronto: The Women's Press, 1985.

Vickers, Jill McCalla, "Where are the Women in Canadian Politics?" *Atlantis*. 3(2, Part II, Spring 1978):40-51.

Vickers, Jill McCalla, "Memoirs of an Ontological Exile: The Methodological Rebellions of Feminist Research," in Angela Miles and Geraldine Finn, eds. *Feminism in Canada*. Montreal: Black Rose Books, 1982.

Vickers, Jill McCalla, *Taking Sex Into Account*. Ottawa: Carleton University Press, 1984.

Wallis, Maria, Wenona Giles, and Carmencita Hernandez, "Defining the Issues on Our Terms: Gender, Race and The State — Interviews with Racial Minority Women," *Resources for Feminist Research*. 17 (3, 1988):43-48.

Warren, Catherine E. *Vignettes of Life: Experiences and Self Perceptions of New Canadian Women*. Calgary: Detselig Enterprises, 1986.

Warskett, Rosemary, "Valuing Women's Work — Dealing with the Limits to State Reform," *Resources for Feminist Research*. 17 (3, September 1988): 67-71.

Weeks, Wendy, "Part-Time Work in Canada: A Study of Ideology and the Implications for Women." M.A. Thesis, McMaster University, Hamilton, 1977.

Weeks, Wendy, "Part-Time Work: The Business View on Second Class Jobs for Housewives and Mothers," *Atlantis* 5 (2, Spring 1980):69-88.

White, Julie, *Women and Unions*. Ottawa: Supply and Services Canada, for the Canadian Advisory Council on the Status of Women, 1980.

White, Julie, *Women and Part-time Work*. Ottawa: Supply and Services Canada, for the Canadian Advisory Council on the Status of Women, 1983.

Wine, Jeri Dawn, "Gynocentric Values and Feminist Psychology," in Angela Miles and Geraldine Finn, eds. *Feminism in Canada*. Montreal: Black Rose Books, 1982.

Women's Liberation Movement, "Brief to the House of Commons Health and Welfare Committee on Abortion Law Reform," in *Women Unite!* Toronto: The Women's Press, 1972.

Wright, Esther Clark, "Women and the State," *Atlantis*. 3 (2, 1977):194-203.

Network Basics Series

- Acheson, Frank & Frost: *Industrialization and Underdevelopment in the Maritimes*
- Armstrong & Armstrong: *Theorizing Women's Work*
- Armstrong, Choiniere, Day: *Vital Signs: Nursing in Transition*
- Buchbinder, Burstyn, Forbes & Steedman: *Who's on Top? The Politics of Heterosexuality*
- Burstyn & Smith: *Women, Class, Family and the State*
- Cohen: *Free Trade and the Future of Women's Work*
- Duffy, Mandell & Puppo: *Few Choices: Women, Work and Home*
- Harman: *When a Hostel Becomes a Home: The Experience of Women*
- Lacombe: *Ideology and Public Policy: The Case Against Pornography*
- Luxton, Rosenberg, Arat-Koç: *Through the Kitchen Window: The Politics of Home and Family, 2nd Enlarged Edition*
- Newson & Buchbinder: *The University Means Business*
- Ng: *The Politics of Community Services*
- Panitch & Swartz: *The Assault on Trade Union Freedoms: From Consent to Coercion, 2nd Edition*
- Tarman: *Privatization and Health Care: The Case of Ontario Nursing Homes*
- Veltmeyer: *Canadian Class Structure*
  Canadian Corporate Power
- White: *The Law, Capitalism and the Right to Work*

Garamond Press, 67A Portland St., Suite 10
Toronto, Ontario M5V 2M9   (416) 597-0246

DATE DUE

Printed by
Marquis, Montmagny, Qc